Entering the Industrial Age

1869–1933

Titles in the Series

From Colonies to a Country 1635–1790

Building the Nation 1791–1832

A Country Divided 1833–1868

Entering the Industrial Age 1869–1933

A World Power 1934 to the Present

DEBATABLE ISSUES
IN U.S. HISTORY

VOLUME FOUR

Entering the Industrial Age

1869–1933

GREENWOOD PRESS
Westport, Connecticut · London

Library of Congress Cataloging-in-Publication Data

Debatable issues in U.S. history / by Creative Media Applications.
        p. cm.—(Middle school reference)
      Includes bibliographical references and index.
ISBN 0–313–32910–9 (set : alk. paper)—ISBN 0–313–32911–7 (v. 1 : alk. paper)—
ISBN 0–313–32912–5 (v. 2 : alk. paper)—ISBN 0–313–32913–3 (v. 3 : alk. paper)—
ISBN 0–313–32914–1 (v. 4 : alk. paper)—ISBN 0–313–32915–X (v. 5 : alk. paper)
    1. United States—History—Miscellanea—Juvenile literature.
2. United States—Politics and government—Miscellanea—Juvenile literature.
3. United States—Social conditions—Miscellanea—Juvenile literature.
4. Critical thinking—Study and teaching (Middle school)—United States.
[1. United States—History. 2. United States—Politics and
government.] I. Creative Media Applications. II. Series.
E178.3.D35   2004
973—dc22   2003056802

British Library Cataloguing in Publication Data is available.

Library of Congress Catalog Card Number: 2003056802
ISBN: 0–313–32910–9 (set)
          0–313–32911–7 (vol. 1)
          0–313–32912–5 (vol. 2)
          0–313–32913–3 (vol. 3)
          0–313–32914–1 (vol. 4)
          0–313–32925–X (vol. 5)

First published in 2004

Greenwood Press, 88 Post Road West, Westport, CT 06881
An imprint of Greenwood Publishing Group, Inc.
www.greenwood.com

Printed in the United States of America

The paper used in this book complies with the Permanent Paper Standard issued by the
National Information Standards Organization (Z39.48–1984).

10 9 8 7 6 5 4 3 2 1

A Creative Media Applications, Inc. Production
Writer: Michael Burgan
Design and Production: Fabia Wargin Design
Editor: Matt Levine
Copyeditor: Laurie Lieb
Proofreader: Betty Pessagno
Indexer: Nara Wood
Associated Press Photo Researcher: Yvette Reyes
Consultant: Mel Urofsky, Professor Emeritus of History at Virginia Commonwealth University

Photo credits:
© PictureHistory *pages* 5, 8, 11, 13, 16, 28, 38, 45, 51, 52, 54, 63, 70, 71
© Hulton Archives/Getty Images *pages* 6, 18, 37, 41, 46, 69, 76, 79, 89, 99, 101, 106
© North Wind Picture Archives *pages* 21, 24, 31, 33, 59
AP/Wide World Photographs *pages* 61, 83, 84, 86, 92, 97, 109, 114, 117, 121, 127, 132

Contents

Introduction 7

CHAPTER ONE: The Election of 1876 11

CHAPTER TWO: The Great Strike of 1877 21

CHAPTER THREE: The Chinese Exclusion Act 31

CHAPTER FOUR: The Haymarket Affair 41

CHAPTER FIVE: *Plessy v. Ferguson* 51

CHAPTER SIX: The Spanish-American War 59

CHAPTER SEVEN: The Industrial Policies of Henry Ford 69

CHAPTER EIGHT: The Coming of World War I 79

CHAPTER NINE: The League of Nations 89

CHAPTER TEN: Prohibition 99

CHAPTER ELEVEN: The Nineteenth Amendment 109

CHAPTER TWELVE: The New Deal 121

Glossary 133

Bibliography 134

Cumulative Index 135

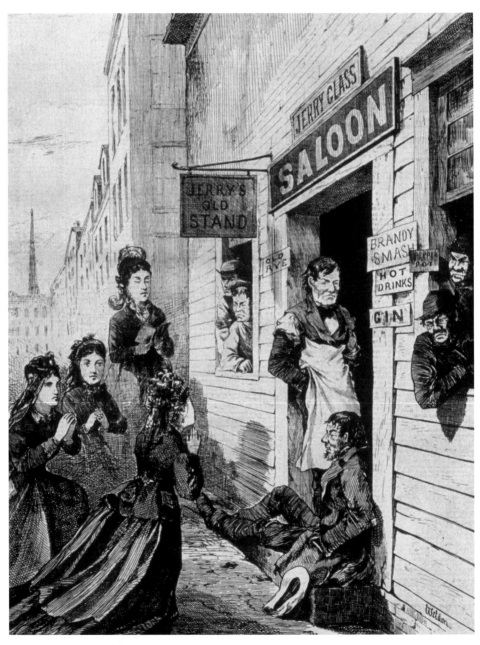

From the start, the United States has been made up of citizens with widely varying views on a range of issues. This newspaper engraving from 1874 shows temperance workers, opposed to drinking alcohol, praying for the patrons of a saloon.

Introduction

*W*hen people come together in a community, they face important decisions about how to run their affairs. Since everyone does not think alike, have the same feelings, or share the same interests, disagreements often arise over key issues.

In a democratic society such as the United States, public debate helps leaders decide what action to take on the most important issues. The debates might start in Congress or another branch of the government. They are often carried on in the media, and they continue in homes, in offices, and wherever concerned citizens gather.

The five volumes of *Debatable Issues in U.S. History* look at some of the most important issues that have sparked political and social debates, from colonial times to the present day. Some of the issues have been local, such as the dispute between Roger Williams and the Puritan leaders of Massachusetts. Williams struggled to introduce the idea of religious freedom in a community that wanted just one kind of religious worship. Other issues—segregation, for example—had special significance for a large group of people. African Americans, who had once been forced to live in slavery, had to endure lingering prejudice even when they received their freedom during and after the Civil War (1861–1865). Some of the most important issues have touched all Americans, as the country's leaders considered whether to go to war in times of international crisis. The 2003 war in Iraq is just the latest example of that debate.

Throughout American history, certain types of issues have appeared over and over. The details may change, but Americans continue to argue over such things as: How much power should

> How much power should the national government have?

the national government have? How does society balance personal freedom with the need to protect the common good? Which political party has the best vision for strengthening the country? Who should America choose as its friends and its enemies around the world?

How does society balance personal freedom with the need to protect the common good?

Historians have debated the importance of certain events for hundreds of years. New facts emerge, or interpretations change as the world changes. From the historians' view, almost any issue is debatable. This series, however, focuses on the events and issues that Americans debated as they occurred. Today, few people would question whether the American colonies should have declared their independence from Great Britain; it seems almost impossible to imagine anything else happening. However, to the Americans of the day, the issue was not so clear-cut. Colonial leaders strongly disagreed on what action to take in the months before Thomas Jefferson wrote the Declaration of Independence.

ANOTHER FAKE WARNING.
—Harding in the Brooklyn *Eagle*.

Copyrighted 1920 by the Star Company.

THE BLIGHT OF EUROPE.
—McCay in the New York *American*.

OPPOSITE VIEWS OF THE ENTANGLEMENT PERIL.

The very formation of the United States took place amid intense debate over new ideas about government, and debate over important issues has continued to be a vital part of American life. The question of whether to join the League of Nations, for instance, the topic of this 1922 political cartoon, was an important debate in the early twentieth century.

At times in the past, debate over key issues might have been limited. From the seventeenth century through most of the nineteenth century, transportation and communication were primitive compared with today. Still, through letters, sermons, newspapers, and government documents, opposing ideas were shared and debated. The lack of electronic communication did not weaken the passion with which people held their beliefs and their desire to shape public issues.

Today, the Internet and other forms of digital communication let millions of people debate crucial issues that face the United States. Better technology, however, does not make it easier for people to settle these issues. As *Debatable Issues in U.S. History* shows, strong emotions often fuel the discussions over the issues. At times, those emotions spill out in violence. On issues that matter most, people are often unwilling to give in, modify their views, or admit that they are wrong. Those attitudes can lead to debates that last for generations. Abortion was a heated issue in 1973, when the U.S. Supreme Court ruled that a woman could legally have an abortion if she chose. Abortion remains a divisive issue today, and there is not much chance that the debate will end.

> Who should America choose as its friends and its enemies around the world?

Debates and disagreements can make it hard for governments to function smoothly. Still, debate allows Americans to explore all sides of an issue. Debate can also lead to new and better ideas that no one had considered before. U.S. Supreme Court Justice William Brennan once noted that Americans have "a profound national commitment to the principle that debate on public issues should be uninhibited, robust, and wide open." That commitment first took shape in colonial America, and it continues today.

A Note to the Reader

The quotations in Debatable Issues in U.S. History *are taken from primary sources, the writings and speeches of the people debating the important issues of their time. Some of the words, phrases, and images in these sources may be offensive by today's standards, but they are an authentic example of our past history. Also, some of the quotes have been slightly changed to reflect the modern spelling of the original words or to make the meaning of the quotes clearer. All metric conversions in this book are approximate.*

CHAPTER ONE

The Election of 1876

WHAT

*Republican Rutherford B. Hayes beats Democrat Samuel Tilden
for the presidency.*

ISSUES

The illegalities of the voting process; the end of Reconstruction

WHERE

Florida, Louisiana, Oregon, and South Carolina

WHEN

1876–1877

*A*braham Lincoln's election as president in 1860 sparked the Civil War (1861–1865). Lincoln's party, the Republicans, wanted to stop the spread of slavery in the United States. Southern slave owners and their supporters decided that they would rather secede, or break apart from the Union, than risk losing slavery. The Republicans' main political opponent, the Democrats, dominated Southern politics at the time. In the North, Democrats split on the war, with some supporting it and some opposing it.

The North's victory in the war gave the Republicans control over Reconstruction, the process of taking the defeated Southern states back into the Union. The Republicans also shaped the legal treatment of freed slaves and African Americans throughout the country. The Republicans fought to pass the Fifteenth Amendment, which gave blacks the right to vote. The Republicans also tried to protect the civil rights of African Americans, in order to guarantee that they received the same treatment as whites in the job market, the schools, and the courts.

The Republicans' concern for African Americans convinced many black voters to join their party. African Americans and some white Northern Republicans who had moved to the South began to dominate politics in the Southern states. At the same time, the Democrats tried to rebuild their strength as a national party. They won support from Americans— both Northerners and Southerners—who opposed the Republicans' policy toward African Americans. During the early 1870s, white Democrats in the South began to redeem, or take back, their old political control. During this process of "Redemption," the whites also tried to take away the legal rights of African Americans. At times, blacks faced violence from whites who did not want blacks to play a meaningful role in Southern society. One Mississippi newspaper reflected the view of many Southerners when it supported "a white man's government, by white men, for the benefit of white men."

Preparing for the 1876 Election

In 1868, Ulysses S. Grant, a Republican, was elected president. During his presidency, some members of his cabinet were accused of crimes. Although Grant had led Union troops to victory during the Civil War, he was not as committed to the goals of Reconstruction as other Republicans, known as Radicals, were. The Radical Republicans made the strongest push to protect the civil rights of blacks. These Republicans also wanted to punish the Southerners who had led the call for secession. However, during Grant's time in office, Americans in general turned away from the Radical Republicans' views on Reconstruction. By the presidential election of 1876, the country was more focused on economic problems, and few Northerners cared how Southern states treated their black citizens.

That year, the Republicans chose Rutherford B. Hayes as their presidential candidate. Hayes had supported the party's position on limiting the spread of slavery. During Reconstruction, he had tended to support the Radicals' plans. In 1876, Hayes did not want former "rebels" controlling the South or the national government. He said that Republicans should ask voters, "Should we give the Government to the men who tried to destroy it?" Yet Hayes also felt that the North and South should try to improve their relations. He did not make Reconstruction his main issue. Instead,

The controversial election of 1876 pitted Rutherford B. Hayes, left, pictured on a campaign poster with his vice presidential running mate, William A. Wheeler, against New York governor Samuel Tilden. Hayes ran as a Republican and Tilden as a Democrat.

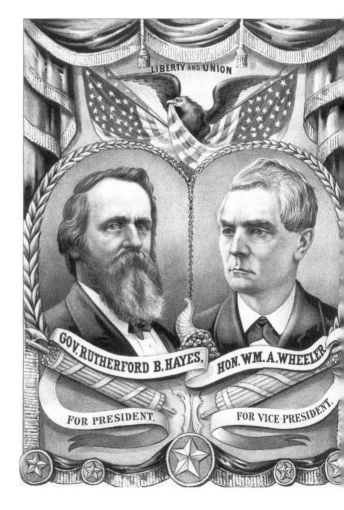

Fast Fact

Starting in 1867,
the U.S. military
took control in
ten Southern states
to enforce
Reconstruction
laws. In 1876, troops
still remained in
Florida, Louisiana,
and South Carolina.

he focused on improving how the government was run, to make sure that the best people received federal jobs.

Hayes's Democratic opponent in 1876 was Samuel Tilden. As governor of New York, Tilden had helped clean up New York City politics. Tilden and the Democrats promised to end corruption in the national government and strengthen the economy, which had weakened during Grant's last years in office. Tilden, a wealthy lawyer, supported the interests of Northern business owners and was likely to win their votes.

In the South, the Democrats had taken back control of every state in the region except Florida, Louisiana, and South Carolina. They used that control to influence the vote. In some cases, the Democrats tried to fool black voters who could not read. The governments created ballots that convinced the voters that they were choosing a Republican while they were actually voting for a Democrat. In the three Republican-controlled states, white Democrats used threats and violence to discourage blacks from voting.

Disputed Results

To win the presidency, a candidate must win a majority of the electoral votes. These votes are awarded by special electors, who are chosen by the voters in each state. The candidate who receives the most votes in a state receives that state's electoral votes. The number of electors matches the total number of representatives and senators that each state sends to Congress. Election results show the total number of voters across the country who have chosen a certain candidate, called the popular vote. More important, however, is the number of states won through their electoral votes.

On election night in 1876, the results showed that Tilden, the Democrat, had won the popular vote, and he had clearly won 184 electoral votes—one short of what he needed for victory. In four states, however, the results were unclear. The three Southern states with Republican governments at first seemed to go for Tilden. Late on election night, however, Daniel Sickles, a Hayes supporter, sent messages to the Republican governors in Florida, Louisiana, and South Carolina. Sickles instructed them to "hold your state" for Hayes. Another Republican leader promised that the government would send those states money and troops to prevent the Democrats from committing any further fraud.

The Republicans claimed that all the disputed electoral votes—a total of twenty—belonged to Hayes. With those votes, he had 185, the exact number needed to win the election. By law, each state had to verify the results of its electoral vote and send them to Congress. In the three Southern states, Republicans controlled this process. They refused to count some popular votes for Tilden, giving Hayes the victory in each state. In the end, those three states and Oregon sent two sets of results to Congress. One set claimed that Hayes had won the electoral votes, while another gave the votes to Tilden. Congress would have to decide which votes to accept.

THE OREGON VOTE

Oregon was the fourth state involved in the 1876 election crisis. One of its three electoral voters was a Republican who planned to support Hayes. The elector, however, was also a government official—he worked for the U.S. Post Office. By law, he should not have been an elector. Oregon's Democratic governor wanted to replace the elector with a Democrat, who would have voted for Tilden.

The fifteen-member electoral commission, pictured in an 1877 illustration, was set up by Congress to make a ruling on the electoral votes sent by Florida, Louisiana, South Carolina, and Oregon after the election of 1876. Questionable voting practices had made it unclear exactly which candidate should receive the electoral votes.

Congress's Solution

The U.S. Constitution says that the results of the electoral vote should be counted in the U.S. Senate. The law, however, does not spell out what to do when a state sends two sets of results. Congress decided to set up a special commission to consider which votes to accept. This Electoral Commission had fifteen members: eight Republicans and seven Democrats.

Congress decided that the Electoral Commission's decisions on the disputed votes would settle the matter, unless both the House and the Senate overruled them. At the time, the House was controlled by Democrats, and the Senate was controlled by the Republicans. Therefore, the House and the Senate were not likely to agree on overturning a ruling from the Electoral Commission. The commission's decision would be the final word on which set of results was accepted.

For each disputed state, the Electoral Commission voted eight to seven in favor of Hayes. Democrats in Congress threatened to delay the vote on accepting the commission's decision, but in the end, they backed down, partly because Republicans had agreed to accept home rule. This meant that each Southern state would decide on its own who would govern it. Reconstruction would end in the South.

By the end of February 1877, Hayes realized that he was about to become president.He wrote in his diary that he was eager "to do what may constitutionally be done to make [the Southern people] again prosperous and happy." He also said that he would uphold the rights of African Americans. However, with the end of Reconstruction, the federal government no longer protected their civil rights. The legal assault on blacks did not end until the civil rights movement of the 1960s.

The Democratic Position on the Election

The Democrats, thinking at first that they had won the election, reacted angrily to the Republican actions in the three Southern states and Oregon. In Louisiana, Tilden had won more votes in the state, but local Republicans controlled the returning board, which carried out the counting process. In the end, the returning board threw out votes that had been cast for both candidates, though Tilden lost thousands more. Tilden lost the electoral votes that he thought he should have won. Democrats accused the Republicans of fraud in Louisiana and the other two Southern states.

From the beginning of the recount process, some Democrats wanted the American people to protest the Republican attempt to "steal" the election. Democratic newspapers called for armed citizens to march on Washington, and one printed the headline "Tilden or War!" Despite these strong words, Tilden held back from attacking Hayes and the Republicans.

Fast Fact

In Florida, the vote was settled by less than 1,000 votes. In the first count, Tilden won by 94 votes. The returning board, however, ruled that Hayes won by 924 votes.

When the Electoral Commission met, Democratic lawmakers argued against the results that favored Hayes. David Dudley Field of New York said that Florida's returning board had acted illegally in throwing out some Democratic votes. The Democrats made similar arguments about the returning boards in Louisiana and South Carolina. The Democrats wanted further investigations of the details of the voting in disputed counties. The findings, they said, would support their claims of fraud. Just four years earlier, the Senate, under Republican control, had carried out a similar study of the Louisiana returning board and rejected its decision, so the state's electoral votes in the 1872 presidential election were not counted.

Supreme Court justice Joseph Bradley, a Republican, held the deciding vote on the commission. He appeared ready to support the Democrats, but then changed his mind and voted for the Republicans. The result meant that Congress would not investigate any alleged fraud in the Southern states. Democrats immediately accused the Republicans of making some kind of deal to win Bradley's vote. One Democratic newspaper said that Bradley was "covered with equal shame and disgrace."

Supreme Court justice Joseph Bradley, pictured in 1870, cast the deciding vote for the Electoral Commission, awarding the presidency to Republican candidate Rutherford B. Hayes in 1877. Angry Democrats assumed that Bradley had made a deal with the Republicans.

In Their Own Words

Samuel Tilden gave a speech after the rulings of the Electoral Commission cost him the presidency. Here is part of what he said.

The question now is whether our elective system, in its substance as well as its form, is to be maintained. This is the question of questions…. It involves the fundamental right of the people. It involves the elective principle. It involves the whole system of popular government. The people must signally condemn the great wrong which has been done to them.

The Republican Position on the Election

To the Republicans, Democratic actions to prevent African Americans from voting were the true crimes of the 1876 election. The returning boards in the three disputed Southern states were simply trying to correct that wrong.

Almost all Republicans backed Hayes and the effort to make him president. Some, however, did admit that the party had acted badly in some of the disputed states. Lew Wallace, a Republican and former Union general, observed the activities in Florida during the recount. He wrote, "If we win, our methods are subject to [legal review] for possible fraud."

Some leading Republicans said that the dealings were not just about helping the Republican Party. If the Democrats won, they feared, the free African Americans of the South would lose their civil rights. If that happened, some Republicans saw new tensions between the North and South, a repeat of the situation before the Civil War. Hayes, however, had often said that he wanted good relations with the Southern states. The fear of future conflicts between the regions may have been overstated.

In front of the Electoral Commission, Republican lawmakers strongly defended the results from the returning boards. They argued that the Constitution gave the states the power to decide election results. Plus, if the commission investigated the results in one county, it would have to repeat the process in every disputed county. By law, the new president had to be chosen by March 4, 1877. The commission did not have enough time to carry out large-scale investigations. With Bradley's vote to accept the results, Hayes and the Republicans won the debate—and the election.

THE ELECTION OF 2000

In some ways, the presidential election of 2000 was similar to the disputed 1876 race. In 2000, Democrat Al Gore won the popular vote but lost the electoral count by just one vote to Republican George W. Bush. Florida's electoral votes decided the election, and the state's process for recounting votes was controlled by local Republicans. In the end, an outside body—the Supreme Court—played a role in the process of awarding the electoral votes.

In Their Own Words

Senator John Sherman of Ohio was one of Hayes's strongest defenders. Here is part of a speech that he gave criticizing the Democrats.

A good deal is said about...fraud and [lying], and wrong. Why, sir, if you go behind the returns in Louisiana, the case is stronger for the Republicans than upon the face of the returns.... While there may have been irregularities, while there may have been a non-observance of some...laws, yet the substantial right was arrived at by the action of the returning board.

CHAPTER TWO

The Great Strike of 1877

WHAT
Railroad workers go on strike, leading to violence.

ISSUES
Pay and conditions for the workers; a worker's right to strike

WHERE
Several major cities, including Baltimore, Maryland; Chicago, Illinois; Pittsburgh, Pennsylvania; and St. Louis, Missouri

WHEN
1877

*I*n 1869, workers from two railroad companies completed a railway that spanned the continent of North America. With this transcontinental line, trains could now travel from the East Coast to the West Coast. The new railway marked the start of a boom in railroad travel, forty years after the first passenger train ran in the United States. The growth of the railroad continued into the next century.

By the 1870s, the railroad companies were the largest industrial employers in the United States. The owners of the companies were some of the wealthiest and most powerful Americans of the day, such as Cornelius Vanderbilt and Thomas Scott. The railroad companies grew with the help of the federal government. The government gave the companies land in the Midwest and the West. The companies then sold some of the land to settlers, using the money to build their lines. The new settlers started farms and businesses that used the railroads to carry their goods.

As towns and cities grew in the West, the railroads brought out even more settlers, who fueled further growth in the towns and the railroad industry. The need for more railways and trains increased the demand for the iron and steel used to build them and for the coal that powered them, helping those industries, as well. In 1882, American poet Walt Whitman called a train the "emblem of motion and power."

> *Fast Fact*
> In 1850, the United States had about 9,000 miles (14,400 kilometers) of railway. By the end of the Civil War in 1865, the country had 35,000 miles (56,000 kilometers) of track. That number almost tripled by 1880.

A Growing Labor Movement

The economic growth that the railroads created also helped build America's labor movement. Since colonial times, workers in the same craft or industry in a particular town or city had sometimes joined together in order to force employers to raise wages or improve working conditions. By forming a group, the workers had more power than if they sought these gains as individuals. They could strike, or refuse to work, if their bosses did not give them what they wanted. A strike was designed to damage the owners' businesses and force them to accept the workers' demands.

By the mid-nineteenth century, workers in one industry who joined together were called a union. Sometimes, local unions from across the country formed a larger, national union. The national unions were still composed of workers in one particular industry. In 1866, however, the National Labor Union (NLU) tried to unite different unions into one "superunion." The increasing interest in unions spread across the country. Railroad workers formed their own unions and sometimes joined the NLU and other national unions that brought together workers from different industries.

Railroad unions sought the same things that other unions fought for: better wages and working conditions. Trains could be dangerous. The steam engines that powered the trains sometimes exploded. Trains sometimes collided or ran off their tracks. One engineer wrote that he could not get a life insurance policy, which would pay his family money if he died. "I did not receive a policy, simply because I was a Locomotive Engineer, which they classified as 'extra hazardous.'" The insurance company figured that the odds were high that the man would be killed on the job.

WORKING ON THE RAILROAD

The railroads created many different types of jobs. Engineers ran the locomotives, the large steam engines that pulled the trains. Firemen shoveled coal into the steam engines to keep them running. Brakemen operated the braking systems that slowed or stopped the trains. Conductors took tickets from the passengers. Switchmen operated the switches on rails that moved trains from one track to another. Other railroad employees supplied water for the steam engines, loaded the goods that the trains carried, and handled communications between the trains and the stations.

Bad Times on the Rails

The railroad industry was the largest industrial employer in the United States in the mid-1800s. Like workers in other industries, railroad workers banded together to form unions. This engraving shows workers laying track on the transcontinental railroad, built in the 1860s.

Pay and conditions worsened on the railroads after 1873. That year, the U.S. economy began to weaken, and the country entered what is called a depression. Companies—especially railroad companies—had spent more money than they had earned and could not pay all their debts. Banks then began refusing to lend money to businesses and individuals, since they were afraid that the loans would not be repaid. Workers received pay cuts or lost their jobs.

As the depression went on, unions in some industries began to strike for higher wages. In general, many unions across the country were suffering, since so many of their members were out of work. In 1877, railroad workers were ready to strike. They had already received one pay cut in 1873, and the major railroad companies put another reduction into effect. The companies were not losing money, but they were not making as much as they had in the past, and some smaller railways were close to going out of business.

In July 1877, workers on the Baltimore and Ohio (B & O) Railroad went out on strike to protest the pay cut. In Baltimore,

Maryland, the company quickly replaced striking workers, but in Martinsburg, West Virginia, the strikers were able to shut down the B & O's operations. Local residents marched to show their support for the strikers. Local militia sent to end the strike also joined the railroad workers' cause, refusing to attack the workers.

Strikes and Violence

West Virginia officials asked President Rutherford B. Hayes to send government troops to Martinsburg. When they arrived, the situation was calm. However, the strike was spreading to other cities, and workers from other railroad companies joined in. In Pittsburgh, Pennsylvania, Pennsylvania Railroad workers refused to run the trains.

On July 21, Pennsylvania's governor sent 600 troops from Philadelphia to Pittsburgh to end the strike because, as in Martinsburg, local militia had refused to act against the strikers. When the Philadelphia troops arrived, they found a crowd who supported the strikers. Some members of the crowd threw rocks at the soldiers. The troops responded by firing their guns, killing about twenty people. A New York reporter wrote, "The sight presented after the soldiers ceased firing was sickening. Old men and boys...lay writhing in the agonies of death." The strikers and their supporters got their own weapons and began to chase the Philadelphia militia before the troops managed to escape the city. An angry crowd of about 20,000 people then set fire to a railroad building and destroyed trains, causing about $5 million worth of damage.

The strikes and riots continued to spread farther west, hitting Chicago, Illinois; St. Louis, Missouri; and San Francisco, California. In St. Louis, workers from other industries briefly went on strike to show their support for the railroad workers. Strike leaders there

Fast Fact

In 1877, an experienced fireman on the B & O Railroad earned about six dollars per week. Today, that salary would be worth about $100.

Fast Fact

After the Pittsburgh strike began, strikers took action again in Baltimore. About ten people died there during labor riots.

were arrested before the situation turned violent. In general, none of the Midwestern and Western cities experienced the violence that Pittsburgh saw. In most cases, local troops were able to prevent damage and end the strikes, though at times, federal troops and local volunteers helped. By the end of July, the strikes were over.

In the long run, the strikes had some benefits for the workers. Starting that October, the railroad companies began to restore the second pay cut and improve working conditions. President Hayes hoped that some government control over the railways would prevent future conflicts.

Famous Figures

THOMAS SCOTT
(1823–1881)

As president of the Pennsylvania Railroad Company, Thomas Scott was a major figure in the Great Strike of 1877. Under Scott, the Pennsylvania Railroad became the largest corporation in America. It owned coal mines and steamships, as well as trains and railways. Scott used his power and political connections to try to win government aid for the railways. The Pennsylvania Railroad was one of several companies hurt by the Great Strike, and Scott wanted President Rutherford B. Hayes to use his influence to end the strike.

The Workers' Position

To the railroad workers, the strikes were their only way to protest their lowered wages. In addition to pay cuts, the workers had to pay their own expenses when they made train trips that lasted overnight. Then they had to pay fares to ride company trains back to their hometowns. Many workers with families could not afford to pay their bills after paying work expenses.

The depression of the era convinced some Americans that the railroad workers were doing the right thing to protect themselves and their families. In New York City, the militia was called out to stop one strike. A soldier said, "Many of us have reason to know what long hours and low pay mean.... We may be militiamen, but we are workmen first."

A Baltimore merchant also understood the workers' reasons for striking. After the strikes in his city, he wrote that the workers received less pay, but the price of goods had not dropped. "The strike," he wrote, "is...a revolt of working men against low prices of labor."

After the strikes, a few newspapers defended the workers. One Chicago paper wrote that for years, the railroad companies had illegally given money to lawmakers to make sure that the federal and state governments would help them grow and let them charge whatever rates they wanted. The pay cuts, the paper wrote, were just the companies' latest attempt to make money by any means necessary. Other papers across the country reported on the public's feelings, which tended to support the workers and the strikes.

In Their Own Words

As the head of the American Federation of Labor (AFL) beginning in 1886, Samuel Gompers became the most powerful union leader in the United States. In his autobiography, Gompers wrote about the importance of the Great Strike.

Made desperate by the accumulation of miseries, without organizations strong enough to conduct a successful strike, the railway workers rebelled. Their rebellion was a declaration of protest... against conditions that [denied] the rights of American citizens. The railroad strike of 1877 was the [alarm bell] that sounded a ringing message of hope to us all.

The railroad workers' strike of 1877 began in Baltimore, Maryland, home of the Baltimore and Ohio (B & O) Railroad, and quickly spread to many other cities, affecting many other railroads. This illustration depicts a scene from the violent strike in Baltimore.

Arguments against the Strikers

Although workers across the country supported the strikers, business owners and the wealthy tended to oppose them. The railroad owners, naturally, did not want to lost money or see their property destroyed in riots. To some Americans, the strikes were illegal, since they limited the companies' legal right to make money by carrying passengers and goods on the railways. Other wealthy Americans saw the strikes as a sign of future conflicts between workers and the government.

For several decades, some industrial workers in Europe had been attracted to a political system called communism. This political system was largely shaped by Karl Marx, a German thinker. Marx said that the working people should unite and take control of the government and the economy. Society as a whole, not private individuals, should own businesses. These ideas opposed the economic system of capitalism, which the United States used.

Capitalism promoted the ownership of private property, and capitalists—such as the railroad owners—wanted as few laws as possible that restricted their actions.

As violence broke out in Pittsburgh and other cities, some Americans thought that communists were organizing the strikes and riots. Just a few years before in Paris, France, communists and other radicals had taken over the city, and they stayed in control until troops drove them out. About 20,000 people died during the violence. Fearing a communist takeover in U.S. cities, some people wanted troops sent in immediately. Thomas Scott said that the workers should get "a rifle diet for a few days and see how they like that kind of bread."

President Hayes had a mixed reaction to the strikes and the calls for federal troops. After the strikes, he wrote that "the [railroad] strikers, as a rule are good men...intelligent and industrious." Yet the president also thought that the strikers were unfairly hurting other workers. "Every man has a right to refuse to work," he wrote, "but no man has a right to prevent others from working." Hayes did not send in as many troops as the railroad companies wanted, but he did send them.

At least one opponent of the strike had no sympathy for the claims that the railroad workers could not live on what they earned. Henry Ward Beecher, a well-known minister in Brooklyn, New York, accused the workers of spending their pay on alcohol and tobacco. He also said that one dollar a day was plenty to buy enough bread and water, and that's all a family needed to live. The *New York Times* reported that Beecher's audience laughed when he said that "the man who cannot live on bread and water is not fit to live."

The Great Strike marked the first time that a strike in one industry spread across the country and that workers in other industries joined in to show their support. The Great Strike was also the first time that federal troops acted to end a strike.

Fast Fact

After the Great Strike, state and local governments began to equip police officers and militia with better weapons, fearing more violent conflicts with workers.

The strike led more workers to form unions and demand better wages and salaries. Most business owners, however, did not want to accept unions or their demands. The Great Strike was just the first of many violent episodes in U.S. labor history.

In Their Own Words

On August 18, 1877, *Harper's Weekly* magazine published an article opposing the Great Strike and the railroad workers. Here is part of that article.

When the men on the Baltimore and Ohio road...resolved that the road should not be used for the transport of freight, they were...stealing as truly as if they had taken to...robbing banks, for they took possession of the property of the corporation and of the merchants who forwarded the freight. They declared that the property of the corporation should be managed as they [the strikers] chose, or not at all, and that the freight should not be directed by its owners, but by them.

CHAPTER THREE

The Chinese Exclusion Act

WHAT
Congress passes a law to end Chinese immigration
to the United States.

ISSUE
The desirability of Chinese immigrants

WHERE
Nationwide, but focused on the West Coast

WHEN
1882

The discovery of gold in California in 1848 set off a gold rush unlike any before in world history. Tens of thousands of people from the United States and other countries flocked to California, hoping to make their fortunes as gold miners. Others came to set up businesses to supply the miners and the settlers who followed them.

Chinese immigrants joined this rush to find wealth and jobs in California. At the time, parts of China faced war and poverty. The promise of gold drew both skilled and unskilled Chinese workers to the United States.

Before 1850, only a few hundred Chinese lived in the United States. During the next three decades, more than 220,000 Chinese—mostly men—arrived in America. About half eventually returned home. Most of the ones who stayed lived in California and nearby states. They often sent money to wives and relatives still living in China.

In the first waves of immigration, most Chinese paid for their own voyages to America. A few had their passage paid by various companies, and in return, the Chinese immigrants worked for the companies in the United States. After working a set number of years—typically seven—a contract worker could leave a company and get a different job.

Fast Fact

The Chinese worked for the Central Pacific Railroad, one of two railroad companies working to build America's first transcontinental railway. The railroad, completed in 1869, linked the east and west coasts of the United States.

Life in California

San Francisco, California, was the center of California's gold boom, and many Chinese settled in that city. The early arrivals created groups to help later Chinese settlers adjust to life in a foreign land. Together, these groups were called the Six Societies or Six Companies. They handled disputes among the Chinese and offered financial and social support.

Some Chinese immigrants prospered during the first years of the gold rush. Men dominated the population of California at this time, and many American men did not want to do jobs associated with women, such as cooking or washing clothes. The Chinese did this work, as well as traditional "male" jobs such as mining and carpentry.

During the 1860s, thousands more Chinese immigrants came to the American West to help build the railroads. Some had skill using the explosives needed to blast away rocks and clear the path for the railway.

Fast Fact

During the gold rush, the Chinese called California "Gold Mountain."

Many Chinese immigrants went to California in the mid-1800s—as did people from other nations and from other parts of the United States—with the dream of getting rich by way of the gold rush. This didn't mean they weren't willing to work hard, however, as these laborers on the Central Pacific Railroad did.

Difficult Times for the Chinese

The Chinese often faced prejudice in California. White Americans controlled U.S. politics and society during the mid-nineteenth century. The Chinese belonged to a different racial group, and most were not Christians, as most Americans were. The sharp rise in Chinese immigration after 1850 alarmed some whites, who disliked all Asians or feared that they would take away jobs from Americans.

During the 1850s and 1860s, California and other Western states passed laws restricting the rights of Chinese residents. In San Francisco, Chinese immigrants could not use the local hospital. In California, Chinese could not become citizens or present evidence in court against whites. Across the state, Chinese children could not go to public schools unless local white parents gave their permission. One white official in California claimed that the attendance of Chinese and African American children would "result in the ruin of our schools."

In 1868, the Burlingame Treaty between the United States and China finally gave Chinese immigrants some legal protection. Among other things, the treaty said that the United States welcomed Chinese immigration and would treat the Chinese in the same way that it treated immigrants from European nations. However, the treaty did not prevent lawmakers in Western states from trying to pass new laws limiting the actions of Chinese immigrants. The lawmakers forced the Chinese to challenge the laws in the courts. The treaty also did not change the racist attitudes of some Americans. During the 1870s, more people began to call for ending all Chinese immigration to the United States.

Starting in 1873, the country entered an economic downturn called a depression. Many businesses could not repay money that they owed banks and investors. Some companies cut salaries, fired workers, or shut down

Fast Fact

The Burlingame Treaty was named for Anson Burlingame, a U.S. diplomat who served in China. The Chinese government respected Burlingame and his skills, so it asked him to represent China in talks with U.S. officials.

completely. In the West, some workers who lost jobs blamed the Chinese for taking jobs that might have gone to whites. A new political party formed to promote the interests of white workers and criticize the Chinese. By 1878, this Workingman's Party was playing a major role in California, helping to pass new anti-Chinese laws.

VIOLENCE AGAINST THE CHINESE

The anti-Chinese feelings in the West sometimes led to violence. At a California mining camp in 1849, white miners attacked Chinese immigrants working for a British company. A much worse attack came in July 1877. Over three days and nights, groups of white men in San Francisco clubbed Chinese with sticks and set fire to their businesses. Military troops and citizens finally combined to stop the attacks. Before this attack, the Six Companies had asked local officials "to protect us to the full extent of your power in all our peaceful, constitutional and treaty rights."

Shutting the Door on Chinese Immigration

The goal of the Workingman's Party was to force all Chinese immigrants out of the United States. As a first step, the party wanted to end the arrival of new immigrants from China. To do that, however, required either ignoring or changing the Burlingame Treaty. Anti-Chinese lawmakers in Congress convinced President Rutherford B. Hayes to meet with China and revise the treaty.

The United States and China signed a new treaty in November 1880. From then on, the United States could suspend the immigration of Chinese workers, but not eliminate it completely. Under the treaty, the U.S. government promised that the Chinese already in the country could "go and come of their own free will." The new treaty also confirmed the legal protections that existing immigrants received under the Burlingame Treaty.

The new treaty went into effect in 1881. Soon, Congress passed the Chinese Exclusion Act, which suspended the immigration of Chinese workers for ten years. The law was specifically meant to keep out workers, both skilled and unskilled. Relatives of Chinese immigrants already in America, however, were allowed to join their families. The Chinese Exclusion Act also said that U.S. courts could not grant citizenship—state or federal—to Chinese immigrants.

PARTY POLITICS AND THE CHINESE

During the 1870s, the Democratic Party in California led the call for restricting Chinese immigration and the rights of Chinese already in the country. Many European immigrants belonged to the party, and they saw the Chinese as a threat to their jobs. As the anti-Chinese feelings grew, the Republicans also began to support exclusion. The Republicans hoped to win the support of voters who disliked the Chinese.

The Arguments for Exclusion

The Chinese Exclusion Act of 1882 reflected long-standing anti-Chinese feelings in America. Although the Chinese lived mostly in the West, the prejudice against them spread across the country. Politicians and newspapers offered many reasons why the Chinese should not be allowed to live in the United States.

Part of the reason was economic. As noted, some American workers believed that companies would hire the Chinese before they hired Americans. In general, the Chinese were willing to accept less pay than Americans and European immigrants. The Chinese were also known to send their money to relatives in China. American merchants complained that the Chinese did not buy as many goods as Americans. When the immigrants did shop, they tended to go to stores owned by other Chinese immigrants, not American shopkeepers. Anti-Chinese Americans saw these shopping habits as part of a larger pattern. In general, the

Chinese seemed to keep to themselves and not try to take part in American society.

Supporters of the exclusion act also claimed that the Chinese were "immoral"—they broke laws, committed acts of violence, gambled, and smoked opium, an illegal drug. One group of workers declared that the Chinese "brought with them nothing but filth, vice, and disease.... All efforts to elevate them to a higher standard have proven [useless]."

Some Americans believed that the Chinese were inferior to whites because God made them that way. Nothing could change their behavior or make them worthy citizens of the United States. In 1876, Congress investigated Chinese immigration. One speaker claimed that "there are none so low" as the Chinese. "I believe that the Chinese have no soul to save, and if they have, they are not worth the saving."

The Workingman's Party was formed during an economic recession when jobs were scarce. Its members, pictured here at an 1879 meeting in front of San Francisco's city hall, felt that the Chinese were to blame for the scarcity of jobs— Chinese workers would work for far lower wages than most, so employers hired them instead of white workers.

A political cartoon from around 1880 perceives the "fear of the period" to be immigrants—Chinese and Irish—devouring Uncle Sam, who represents the United States. The solution suggested here is for the immigrants to devour each other.

In Their Own Words

Dennis Kearney was the founder of the Workingman's Party, which led the effort against the Chinese. Here is part of a speech that he gave in 1878.

These cheap slaves [the Chinese] fill every place…. The father of a [white] family is met by them at every turn. Would he get work for himself? Ah! A stout Chinaman does it cheaper. Will he get a place for his oldest boy? He cannot. His girl? Why, the Chinaman is in her place too! Every door is closed….

California must be all American or all Chinese. We are resolved that it shall be American, and are prepared to make it so.

The Arguments against Exclusion

Americans who opposed the Chinese Exclusion Act had both economic and legal reasons. Business owners and their supporters in Congress wanted a steady supply of workers. For most of America's history, businesses lacked enough workers to fill all the jobs available. Immigrants, both skilled and unskilled, helped meet that need. Without immigrant labor, companies had to pay more to Americans to fill the jobs, pushing up their costs.

Some lawmakers opposed an early version of the exclusion act because they felt that it violated the 1880 treaty with China. The treaty allowed the U.S. government to suspend Chinese immigration for a "reasonable" time. Twenty years, the lawmakers argued, was too long to be considered reasonable. Representative Charles Joyce of Vermont said that he would not support the law even if the time period was for one hour. To him, the law was "a bold and open violation" of the 1880 treaty.

A few Americans believed that the Chinese Exclusion Act unfairly attacked the Chinese. These people defended the Chinese as generally hardworking and honest. A few opponents also saw that racism was at work. Senator Joseph Hawley of Connecticut said, "An exclusion based upon race or color is unphilosophical, unjust and undemocratic." Another senator opposed using race as one of the conditions for becoming a citizen. Some critics of exclusion had earlier pointed out that denying the Chinese citizenship would make them less likely to play a role in American society. In this way, the exclusion law would reinforce what anti-Chinese Americans disliked about the immigrants—that they did not become politically active.

Fast Fact

According to the 2000 U.S. Census, more than 1.3 million residents of the United States were born in China. That year, slightly more than 50,000 Chinese immigrants entered the country.

The opponents of the Chinese Exclusion Act could not stop it from becoming law. The 1882 law marked the first time that the U.S. government limited immigration from a particular country. When the Chinese Exclusion Act was repealed in 1943, a new system allowed only a certain number of Chinese immigrants per year. After 1965, this quota system ended, and Chinese immigrants arrived in America in large numbers, as they had in the decades after the gold rush.

In Their Own Words

Harper's Weekly magazine opposed the Chinese Exclusion Act. Here is part of an editorial from 1882 that attacked the law.

Considering the traditional declaration of our pride and patriotism that America is the home for the oppressed of every clime and race, considering the spirit of our constitutional provision that neither race, color, nor previous condition of servitude shall bar a citizen from voting, is it not both monstrous and ludicrous to decree that American civilization is endangered by the "[Chinese] invasion?"

CHAPTER FOUR

The Haymarket Affair

WHAT
*Eight men are convicted of murder after
violence breaks out at a labor rally.*

ISSUES
*The guilt of the convicted men;
the role of the labor movement in U.S. society*

WHERE
Chicago, Illinois

WHEN
1886

BE UNITED

INDUSTRIOUS

AMALGAMATED SOCIETY OF ENGINEERS, MACHINISTS, MILLWRIGHTS,
SMITHS, AND PATTERN MAKERS.

This is to Certify that   was admitted a Member of the

*D*uring the nineteenth century, new industries developed in Europe and the United States. These included the railroads, steel manufacturing, and food packing. At the same time, old industries, such as coal mining, grew. During this Industrial Revolution, large numbers of people began working in factories for the first time. Most faced long hours and difficult conditions. Meanwhile, many of the investors who owned the largest companies became millionaires. They enjoyed good relations with politicians, who often promoted their companies' interests.

Fast Fact

As a group, workers are called labor. Business owners are known collectively as capitalists, or simply capital—the same word used to describe the money that they spent to start their businesses.

The growth of industry led to the rise of labor unions. Workers joined together in unions to fight for better wages and working conditions. By forming a group, the workers had more power than if they sought these gains as individuals. They could strike, or refuse to work, if their bosses did not give them what they wanted. A strike was designed to damage the owners' businesses and force them to accept the workers' demands.

The effort to create labor unions was influenced by socialism. This economic system was based on ideas developed by several different thinkers. One of the most important was Karl Marx. He called for a form of socialism that he called communism. He urged workers to rise up against the capitalists and take control of the factories. The workers would then own the factories and be their own bosses.

In the United States, socialists often led the effort to form the first labor unions. Many of the socialists came from Europe—particularly Germany. They moved to cities that had large factories and many industrial workers, such as Chicago, Illinois. Some socialists wanted to focus on economic issues, such as building the strength of unions. Others stressed political activity, such as electing officials who would support their views. A small number of socialists wanted to use violence to overthrow the business owners and the political system altogether. These radical labor figures were called anarchists. Most anarchists believed that no person or group of people should limit another person's freedom.

Famous Figures

KARL MARX
(1818–1883)

To many workers, Karl Marx was a hero. To many capitalists, he stood for a political system that threatened their right to own private property. With Friedrich Engels, Marx took the ideas of many different political and social thinkers and used them to create a political theory that is sometimes called Marxism. The two men worked together on one of the most widely read books of all time, *The Communist Manifesto,* published in 1848.

Marx believed that throughout history, people fell into different groups, or classes, based on the roles that they played in the economy. In the industrial age, factory workers would lead a violent revolution to end the power of the capitalists and create a classless society. Everyone as a whole, not individuals, would own property. Marx's ideas were first put into practice in Russia, where a communist revolution occurred in 1917, creating the Soviet Union. For decades, communist leaders killed millions of their own citizens who opposed government policies. In 1991, Soviet citizens' hatred of those policies and pressure from the United States finally led to the end of communism in Russia. Only a few countries currently use Marxist ideas to run their societies.

The Haymarket Violence

In 1886, the main labor issue was the eight-hour workday. At the time, most people worked ten hours or more each weekday, with extra hours on Saturday. They were paid by the day, not the hour, so working more hours in a day did not earn them more money.

In Chicago, anarchists worked with socialists and nonsocialist union members to promote the eight-hour workday. On May 1, the different labor groups called for a rally to demand the right to work no more than eight hours per day. Before the rally, anarchist newspapers in the city had called for using violence to smash the capitalist system. "One pound of DYNAMITE," one paper wrote, "is better than a bushel of BALLOTS!"

However, the protests were peaceful. Albert Parsons, a leading anarchist, led a parade of about 80,000 people through the city. August Spies, another important anarchist, wrote an article praising the rally. It said, "Workmen, let your watchword be: No Compromise!"

On May 3, violence broke out at the McCormick Reaper Works in Chicago, where a strike was under way. Some of the strikers, as well as union members, battled the workers that McCormick had hired to take their jobs. Police arrived to end the riot and killed several unarmed workers. When Spies heard about the deaths, he immediately wrote a plea to other workers. He wanted them to protest the killings of the workers who, "like you, had the courage to disobey the supreme will of your bosses."

The next evening, Chicago workers held a rally at Haymarket Square. The labor press had told the workers to bring weapons, but Spies told the crowd that they were not ready yet to carry out violence. Parsons spoke also, saying only that socialism would help the workers live better lives.

Around ten o'clock, most of the workers left the square. The last speaker, Samuel Fielden, told the small crowd that remained that it should resist "the law"—the police that protected the interests of the business owners. These words led to the arrival of about 200 police officers, who had been stationed nearby. One officer told the crowd to leave, and Fielden said that they would. Suddenly, a bomb exploded in front of the police. A few officers were knocked down, and the rest began firing their guns and swinging their clubs at the workers. One Chicago paper reported that the officers "were blinded by passion and unable to distinguish between the peaceable citizen and the...assassin." When the violence ended, one officer was dead, and six others later died of their wounds from the bomb blast. At least four civilians were killed in the violence after the explosion. Dozens more were injured in what became known as the Haymarket Affair.

Although the first speakers at the labor rally at Chicago's Haymarket Square urged those assembled to avoid violence, inflammatory comments later in the program caused the police to intervene, and violence erupted nonetheless. This magazine illustration shows the bomb exploding in front of the police.

A worker from the Amalgamated Society of Engineers carried this union card from the mid-1800s as proof of his membership. Another word for "amalgamated" is "united."

Trial and Execution

Almost immediately, Chicago police began hunting for the radicals who had planned the bomb attack. Eventually, ten anarchists were charged with the murder of a Chicago police officer and several other offenses. One of the ten escaped and was never brought to trial. Another provided evidence against the others and was not brought to court. The eight who stood trial were

Spies, Parsons, Fielden, Adolph Fischer, George Engel, Louis Lingg, Oscar Neebe, and Michael Schwab. All except Parsons and Neebe were immigrants.

Julius Grinnell was the prosecutor—the lawyer who argued the state's case against the anarchists. He never produced evidence that linked any of the men to the bomb. Six of them proved that they were not even at Haymarket Square at the time of the bombing. Still, on December 3, 1886, the jury found all eight men guilty and sentenced seven of them to be hanged. (Neebe received a fifteen-year prison sentence.)

Legal appeals went unheeded. Four of the eight—Parsons, Spies, Fischer, and Engel—were hanged on November 11, 1887. Lingg killed himself before the execution. Schwab and Fielden had their sentences reduced to jail time. They and Neebe were pardoned six years later by Illinois governor John Peter Altgeld.

Against the Anarchists

In 1886, most Americans did not care for the ideas of socialists and anarchists. Even many workers rejected their arguments. The Haymarket Affair stirred anger among Americans who supported capitalism—the economic system of the United States—and wanted law and order. Newspaper publishers, lawmakers, business owners, and ministers led the attacks on the men accused in the Haymarket bombing.

The feelings against the anarchists also reflected a fear and hatred of foreigners. Immigration to the United States grew sharply after the Civil War (1861–1865). Business owners usually welcomed immigrants because they provided cheap labor, but the capitalists did not like the radical ideas that some workers brought with them to America. To the owners, unions and the calls for an eight-hour day were foreign ideas that threatened their business interests.

Some native-born Americans believed that foreigners took away their jobs. Also, since many immigrants would accept lower pay than native-born Americans, business owners could keep wages low for all workers. Some Americans favored restricting immigration. One New York City paper claimed that this would keep out "foreign savages."

During the Haymarket trial, Julius Grinnell drew upon the strong feelings against socialism, anarchism, and foreigners. He called on witnesses who had heard some of the anarchists talking about using violence to achieve their aims. He also showed articles that the men had published urging violence. Grinnell convinced the jury that the anarchists, with their words, had encouraged someone to throw the bomb on May 4—the accused were "as guilty as the individual who in fact threw it."

The judge in the case, Joseph Gary, helped Grinnell make his case. After Grinnell and the lawyers for the anarchists presented their evidence, Gary gave final instructions to the jury. The judge told the jury that it did not matter who actually threw the bomb; if the anarchists' words had indeed led to that action, they were just as guilty.

In Their Own Words

Here is part of Julius Grinnell's closing argument to the jurors in the Haymarket trial.

Law is on trial. Anarchy is on trial. These men have been selected, picked out by the grand jury and [accused] because they were leaders. They are no more guilty than the thousands who follow them. Gentlemen of the jury, convict these men, make examples of them, hang them and you save our institutions, our society.

The Anarchists' Defense

In the court, the anarchists admitted that they had spoken out against police officers. They did not deny that they had encouraged workers to arm themselves. However, the anarchists denied that they had suggested someone throw a bomb at the Haymarket rally, and they insisted that they had nothing to do with the violence that erupted on May 4. They suggested that someone working with the police might have thrown the bomb to give the officials an excuse to arrest and execute anarchist leaders.

The anarchists and their lawyers turned to the U.S. Constitution for their legal defense. The First Amendment gave them the right to speak or publish anarchist ideas. That amendment also gave them the right to meet with other anarchists and socialists and discuss their ideas. The lawyers argued that Grinnell had turned the trial into a legal debate on the anarchists' beliefs, not on whether they took part in the killing on May 4.

During and after the trial, other socialists and anarchists attacked how Grinnell argued the case. They accused him of trying to use the emotions of the jury and the community to convict innocent men. Dyer Lum, an anarchist, wrote that "fear paralyzed reason, and force—arbitrary and illegal—held sway."

The anarchists also received support from people who did not agree with their political ideas. William Dean Howells, a noted author, called the anarchists' beliefs "unthinkable," yet he thought that the men had not received a fair trial.

The opinions of Howell and other respected Americans did not stop the executions, but did influence Governor Altgeld's decision to pardon Neebe, Fielden, and Schwab. After studying the case, the governor said that the trial had been flawed from the beginning. Grinnell and Gary had not acted properly, and no evidence linked the accused men with the bombing. Altgeld said that it was his duty to pardon the anarchists because of all the legal errors.

The Haymarket Affair showed how strong the fear of radical ideas was during the late nineteenth century. No one could deny that someone had thrown a bomb that killed a police officer and that the anarchists had called for violence in the past. In this case, however, the law was stretched to convict men who held beliefs that most Americans did not accept.

In Their Own Words

In court, the eight accused men proclaimed their innocence. Here is part of Albert Parsons's speech in court.

I am an innocent man.... I am simply the victim of...those whose anger has been aroused by the power...of the labor organizations of America.... I am ready, if need be, to lay down my life for the rights of my fellowmen. But I object to being killed on false and unproven accusations.... I have not been proven guilty. I leave it to you to decide from the record itself as to my guilt or innocence.

THE HAYMARKET MONUMENT

Lucy Parsons led an effort to build a monument for her husband Albert and the other executed anarchists. The Haymarket Monument was unveiled just before Governor Altgeld pardoned the three survivors in 1893. It features a statue of a woman who represents Justice, drawing a sword as she stands above a dead worker. The woman symbolizes justice for all workers. Also on the monument are the last words of August Spies: "The day will come...." The Haymarket Monument still stands in Chicago's Forest Home Cemetery.

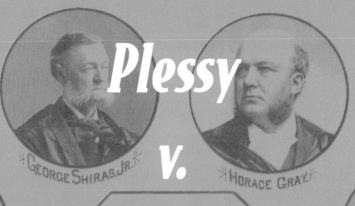

CHAPTER FIVE

Plessy

v.

Ferguson

GEORGE SHIRAS JR.

HORACE GRAY.

STEPHEN J. FIELD.

RUFUS W. PECKHAM.

DAVID J. BREWER.

CHIEF JUSTICE FULLER.

WHAT

Homer Plessy challenges a law that separates
African Americans and whites on trains.

EDWARD D. WHITE.

ISSUE

The legality of "separate but equal" public spaces for
African Americans and whites

WHERE

Louisiana

WHEN

1896

HENRY B. BROWN.

JOHN M. HARLAN.

JUSTICES OF THE

United States Supreme Court.

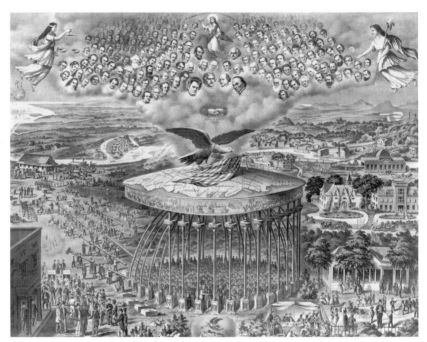

This fanciful illustration from 1867 uses both religious and patriotic imagery to depict the reconciliation of the North and South after the Civil War through the federal program of Reconstruction. An ambitious program, Reconstruction had only limited success in meeting its goals.

ith the end of the Civil War (1861–1865), the United States entered a period known as Reconstruction. The country's leaders wanted to rebuild the defeated South. Many also wanted to help freed slaves gain their legal and political rights. But the end of slavery did not end racist beliefs.

Many Southern states passed new laws known as "Black Codes." According to these codes, criminals who could not pay fines were required to perform hard labor. The law targeted poor blacks. Black Codes also kept African Americans from serving on juries or giving testimony in court against whites. In some states, the codes also forced freed slaves to sign contracts with their employers in order to receive jobs.

In response to the Black Codes, Congress and the states passed three amendments to the Constitution. The Thirteenth Amendment outlawed slavery across the country. The Fourteenth Amendment gave African Americans U.S. citizenship and limited the states' ability

Fast Fact

Before Reconstruction, free blacks in the North often faced discrimination. The new amendments of the 1860s protected their rights, as well as those of the newly freed Southern slaves.

to pass laws that denied anyone—especially blacks—their civil rights. The Fifteenth Amendment prevented states from denying a person's right to vote based on race. Congress also passed other laws that protected the rights of African Americans.

Civil Rights and Segregation

The Black Codes also tried to segregate blacks and whites (keep them separate) in public places such as hotels, restaurants, and railroads. The new amendments had some effect in limiting segregation, but Southern leaders kept trying to create separate spaces for blacks and whites. Laws aimed at increasing segregation were sometimes called "Jim Crow" laws. The name referred to an African American character played by white actors in musical performances called minstrel shows.

In 1875, Congress passed the Civil Rights Act to end segregation. Many Southerners opposed the act and challenged it in court. In 1883, the U.S. Supreme Court ruled that the act was unconstitutional. The law tried to extend the Fourteenth Amendment's legal protection to private places and acts, but the Court said that the amendment only applied to any state actions that denied civil rights. The Court also said that the federal government could not protect freed blacks in every part of life but only in areas directly related to their political rights. Justice Joseph Bradley wrote that the time had come for freed blacks to be "mere citizen[s]" and not "the special favorite[s] of the law."

By this time, Reconstruction had ended in the South. Congress and many Northerners were willing to let the Southern states pass whatever laws they chose regarding African Americans. The Supreme Court's action on the Civil Rights Act of 1875 confirmed the South's ability to pass new Jim Crow laws.

Fast Fact

The concept behind Jim Crow laws was called "equal but separate" in Louisiana and other Southern states, but today, it is usually called "separate but equal."

Fast Fact

The Civil Rights Act of 1875 was the last major U.S. law designed to protect the rights of African Americans until the civil rights movement of the 1950s and 1960s.

In some states, the law called for "equal but separate" facilities for blacks and whites. In reality, however, the spaces set aside for blacks were often less comfortable than the ones for whites.

Plessy Challenges Jim Crow

A group of African Americans in Louisiana decided to challenge the "equal but separate" policy on the state's trains. They selected Homer Plessy to purchase a ticket and ride in a whites-only train car.

Plessy boarded the train on June 7, 1892. His arrest was already arranged with railroad officials, since Plessy was light-skinned and could have passed as a white. The group supporting him wanted to make sure that Plessy was arrested as an African American who tried to sit in the car reserved for whites.

Plessy's legal team included Albion Tourgée, a white New York writer and attorney who supported equal rights for African Americans. Plessy's lawyers argued that the Louisiana "equal but separate" law for trains violated the Constitution. Since the law was unconstitutional, Plessy's trial should not continue. John Ferguson, the judge hearing the case, disagreed.

Plessy's lawyers asked the state supreme court to review its arguments. This court also ruled that the trial should continue. Finally, Tourgée and his team asked the U.S. Supreme Court to step in and hear the state court's ruling. Plessy's lawyers said that the Louisiana court had failed to follow proper legal rules in its decisions.

The designation "Jim Crow," originally the name of an African American character in minstrel shows, referred to the Black Codes and other segregation laws enacted in the South after Reconstruction. This illustration of Jim Crow dates from the 1870s.

The Supreme Court Decision

The Supreme Court finally heard *Plessy v. Ferguson* in April 1896. Once again, Plessy's attorneys argued that Plessy's constitutional rights were denied by Louisiana law. Lawyers representing Judge Ferguson and the state of Louisiana said that the law was constitutional. In the end, the Court ruled for Ferguson in a seven-to-one decision. (One of the nine justices did not vote.)

In the South, most people welcomed the decision. A Virginia law journal wrote with approval that the decision meant that segregation was legal in all public places. In the North, however, some papers criticized the Supreme Court's ruling. A New York City paper wrote, "It is unfortunate...that our highest court has declared itself in opposition to the effort to [remove] race lines in State legislation."

Fast Fact

Jim Crow laws remained legal until 1954, when the U.S. Supreme Court ruled in *Brown v. Board of Education of Topeka, Kansas*, that separate but equal laws did violate the constitutional rights of African Americans.

The Arguments
against the Louisiana Law

Tourgée focused his legal arguments on the Thirteenth and Fourteenth Amendments. The Thirteenth Amendment outlawed slavery. Tourgée said that slavery should include any system that denied the rights of one group of people based on race and gave another group power over the first group.

The key part of Tourgée's case rested on the Fourteenth Amendment. That amendment granted citizenship to all people born in the country. Citizenship, Tourgée, said, applied equally to everyone. Louisiana was unfairly singling out black riders by placing them in separate train cars. Also, state citizenship sprang from national citizenship—the two were not separate. That relationship, Tourgée argued, gave the national government the power to step in and stop state efforts to take away the rights that come with citizenship.

The Fourteenth Amendment also guarantees every American "due process." This means that proper, known rules must be followed if a government or person tries to take away an American's "life, liberty, or property." On the Louisiana trains, the conductors decided on their own if riders were black or white. The riders had no formal way to prove that their actual racial background differed from the conductors' opinions. This, Tourgée said, denied African Americans due process.

Tourgée claimed that Plessy and other blacks were also denied their right to equal protection, another guarantee in the Fourteenth Amendment. The Louisiana law made exceptions for some blacks riding in white cars, such as nurses traveling with white children. That distinction, Tourgée said, showed that the law was really about keeping blacks beneath whites in social status. Black nurses worked for whites, so they were acceptable in white cars, but blacks who were assumed to be equal to whites were not allowed in the cars.

John Marshall Harlan was the only justice on the Court who accepted some of Tourgée's arguments and voted for Plessy. In his dissenting opinion regarding *Plessy v. Ferguson*, Harlan, borrowing one of Tourgée's phrases, wrote, "Our Constitution is color-blind and neither knows nor tolerates classes among citizens."

In Their Own Words

Here is part of Justice John Marshall Harlan's dissent in *Plessy v. Ferguson.*

What can more certainly arouse race hate...than state [laws] which, in fact, proceed on the ground that colored citizens are so inferior and degraded that they cannot be allowed to sit in public coaches occupied by white citizens[?]... The sure guarantee of the peace and security of each race is the clear...recognition...of...the equality before the law of all citizens of the United States, without regard to race.

The Case against Plessy

Milton J. Cunningham, the state's attorney general, wrote a legal brief said that denying Plessy the right to use a certain railroad car did not treat him as if he were a slave, even though the denial was based on race. In that case, Tourgée's argument about a violation of the Thirteenth Amendment was wrong. Louisiana officials also believed that separating blacks and whites in public places would prevent conflicts between the two races. Another lawyer, Alexander Peter Morse, argued that the Fourteenth Amendment did not limit a state's ability to use its police powers to protect public order and prevent violence in this way.

Regarding the issue of due process, Cunningham claimed that in most cases, a conductor could tell if a rider was white or black. The brief stated, "As a rule...it requires no exercise of judicial powers to determine that question." Therefore, Plessy had not been denied due process.

The Supreme Court accepted many of these arguments. Justice Henry Billings Brown wrote the majority opinion for the Court. He said that the Thirteenth Amendment only applied if a state were trying to reintroduce slavery, which was not an issue in *Plessy*. On the equal protection issue, he said that separating blacks and whites in public did not mean Louisiana was claiming that one race was better or had more rights than the other.

Brown also said that the Fourteenth Amendment applied to political or legal equality, but not social equality. Underlying Brown's opinion was his belief that the white and black races had natural differences and inequalities. He believed that laws and the Constitution could not change that condition, which many white Americans accepted as a fact.

In Their Own Words

Here is part of Justice Henry Billings Brown's opinion for the Supreme Court.

[Plessy's] argument...assumes that social prejudices may be overcome by legislation, and that equal rights cannot be secured to the negro except by an enforced [mixing] of the two races. We cannot accept this proposition. If the two races are to meet upon terms of social equality, it must be the result of...a mutual appreciation of each other's merits and a voluntary consent of individuals.

CHAPTER SIX

The Spanish-American War

WHAT
The United States defeats Spain and takes control
of several Spanish colonies.

ISSUES
The need for the war; the desirability of owning colonies

WHERE
Nationwide

WHEN
1898

*T*hroughout the nineteenth century, some American political leaders eyed Cuba as a possible colony for the United States. The island, which sits just 90 miles (144 kilometers) south of Florida, was a major source of sugar. In 1854, some U.S. officials wanted to buy Cuba from Spain—or take it by force, if the Spanish refused to sell. That plan, however, was never acted on, and Cuba remained in Spanish hands.

By the 1890s, some U.S. businesses had growing investments in the Cuban sugar industry. Americans also took an interest in Cuba's attempt to win its independence from Spain. In 1895, Cubans based in New York organized a revolution against the Spanish government. Cuban rebels burned sugar fields, trying to take away Spain's main source of income on the island.

A few U.S. newspapers closely covered the events in Cuba. They tried to show that the Cubans were bravely fighting for liberty against a country that denied them their rights. These papers helped build support for the rebels and led the call for the United States to take an active role in the revolution. President Grover Cleveland, however, did not want the country to go to war with Spain. He opposed the rebels, yet he also wanted Spain to grant the island more freedom in running its own affairs.

YELLOW JOURNALISM

Two New York newspapers, the *Journal* and the *World,* led the attack on Spain in their articles. The *Journal* was owned by William Randolph Hearst, who also owned other newspapers across the country. Joseph Pulitzer owned the *World.* Today, an important award given to journalists and artists is named for him. During the 1890s, Pulitzer and Hearst battled to build the most successful paper in New York City. Their reports on the Cuban rebellion were part of that struggle, as each tried to stir strong feelings in their readers, sometimes by distorting or making up facts. This kind of journalism came to be called "yellow journalism." The name comes from a comic strip that ran in the *Journal,* "The Yellow Kid," which was printed in yellow ink.

Although President William McKinley wanted to avoid war with Spain, he showed some support for Cuban rebels by sending the U.S. battleship Maine *to Cuba's Havana Harbor. The ship mysteriously blew up on February 5, 1898. The loss of the* Maine *and more than 250 sailors aboard sparked public support of a war with Spain.*

The Road to War

In 1897, William McKinley became the twenty-fifth president of the United States. He followed Cleveland's policies on Cuba—he did not want to recognize the rebels as the true government in Cuba. McKinley believed that recognition could lead to war with Spain. Still, he seemed to have more concern for the rebels than Cleveland had. McKinley had received reports that the Spanish government was using brutal measures against civilians as it tried to regain control of the island.

At the same time, Spain was trying to make reforms that would give Cuba more local control. To the Cubans, however, the changes were not good enough. In January 1898, riots broke out in the capital of Havana as residents protested the proposed reforms. Soon after, McKinley sent the battleship *Maine* to Havana to show U.S. concern over the violence there.

Fast Fact

Americans who owned sugar fields in Cuba sometimes paid the rebels money so that the fighters would not torch their fields. The rebels then used this money to finance their revolution.

A few weeks later, U.S. newspapers published a letter written in 1897 by Enrique Dupuy de Lôme, a Spanish diplomat. Cuban rebels had somehow acquired the letter and passed it on to the Americans. De Lôme called President McKinley "weak" and a "would-be politician." The letter also suggested that Spain was not serious about reforming its policies in Cuba or peacefully ending the rebellion. De Lôme's letter angered McKinley and stirred anti-Spanish feelings across the country.

The crisis deepened just a few days later when the *Maine* mysteriously blew up in Havana's harbor. More than 250 U.S. sailors died, and the press and some politicians blamed Spain for the explosion. More Americans demanded a war with Spain to end the violence in Cuba and avenge the dead sailors. "Remember the *Maine!*" became a popular slogan. In March, Congress approved $50 million for new weapons.

In April, McKinley asked Congress to declare war on Spain. He said that the United States had to act to end the revolution, which was killing Cuban civilians and threatening U.S. interests on the island. Congress declared that Cuba was independent, though the U.S. government still refused to recognize the rebels as the true government. McKinley and others believed that the United States would first have to help the Cubans build a democratic government. At the same time, U.S. lawmakers declared that the United States did not want to annex Cuba (take control of it as a colony).

"A Splendid Little War"

Thousands of young American men rushed to volunteer to fight against Spain. The first troops left Florida for Cuba in June. By then, the United States had already won a great victory at sea. A U.S. fleet led by

Admiral George Dewey destroyed a Spanish fleet near Manila, the capital of the Philippines. Those Pacific islands were also part of Spain's colonial empire. Dewey was carrying out a military plan drafted long before the war. The United States had growing economic interests in Asia, and the U.S. Navy had already considered the Philippines as a potentially valuable base for its ships.

In Cuba, U.S. troops worked with the rebels to defeat the Spanish. The heaviest fighting took place around the city of Santiago, where soldiers known as the Rough Riders helped defeat the Spanish. Theodore Roosevelt was one of the commanders of this volunteer unit. (After the war, in 1900, he was elected vice president.) Also playing a key role at Santiago were the Ninth and Tenth Cavalries, comprised of African American soldiers. After the land battle, the U.S. Navy won another major victory, defeating the Spanish in Santiago's port. A few weeks later, U.S. troops took control of Puerto Rico, another Spanish colony in the region.

Future president Theodore Roosevelt can be seen in the center of this picture in the light-colored shirt. He was one of the commanders of the Rough Riders, a volunteer unit that saw heavy fighting in Santiago, Cuba, during the Spanish-American War. Roosevelt would serve as president from 1901 to 1909.

One U.S. diplomat called the Spanish-American War (1898) a "splendid little war." But by the middle of August, Spain was ready to end the war. The Americans, who won without losing many soldiers, quickly achieved what they wanted. Spain granted Cuba its independence, and the United States would play a role in shaping the new government. Spain also agreed to give the United States Puerto Rico, the Philippines, and Guam, a small island in the Pacific Ocean.

HARDSHIPS ON THE BATTLEFIELD

Of the more than 5,400 American troops who died during the Spanish-American War, only 379 were killed in combat. The rest died from sickness or accidents. The Americans in Cuba were exposed to deadly diseases, such as yellow fever and malaria. Drugs used today to fight those illnesses were not available in 1898.

For War and Empire

The Spanish-American War came at a time when some Americans believed that the United States should take a larger role in world affairs. Europe's most powerful countries—especially Great Britain, France, and Germany—had overseas empires or were actively seeking to expand their international trade. In this era of imperialism, Americans wanted to increase their global economic activity, particularly in Asia. To do that, the country needed bases for its navy, which would protect U.S. shipping and citizens living abroad.

Creating an empire was also seen as part of America's "Manifest Destiny." That phrase had first been used in the 1840s, when some Americans wanted to take control of California and other lands that were then part of Mexico. Manifest Destiny meant that the United States had a God-given right to grow and to spread democracy. During the 1880s and 1890s, this idea some-times had a racial tone. Josiah Strong, a minister, suggested in 1885 that the white race that developed in Great Britain and settled America had special talents. These talents meant that Americans had a duty to influence or control people of other races around the world.

One of the leading supporters of American impe-rialism was Henry Cabot Lodge, a Republican senator from Massachusetts. In 1895, Lodge wrote that other nations were planning for the future by taking control of distant lands. The United States, he said, "as one of the great nations of the world, must not fall out of the line of the march."

Lodge also had an interest in Cuba and its rebel-lion. He and others believed that an independent Cuba would benefit U.S. business interests on the island. Ending Spanish rule there might also weaken Spain. Then the United States would be in a better position to expand its trade wherever Spain lost influence.

> *Fast Fact*
> The United States acquired its first Pacific colony while still at war with Spain. In July 1898, the U.S. government annexed the Hawaiian Islands.

Not everyone who supported the war was an imperialist. Some Americans were genuinely concerned about the suffering of the Cuban people. War with Spain seemed like the only way to end the violence on the island and to give the people greater freedom. Other war supporters felt that the United States had to defend its honor after the de Lôme letter and the sinking of the *Maine*.

Once the war was over, American imperialists wanted the United States to take over former Spanish colonies. The Philippines gave the country an excellent base in the Pacific Ocean. The residents there would buy U.S. goods, as well, and the islands could supply natural resources for U.S. businesses. The Philippines were also close to China, which was the true target of U.S. economic expansion in Asia. Europeans were already in China, and the United States hoped to play a role there in the future.

Famous Figures

HENRY CABOT LODGE
(1850–1924)

A member of a rich, powerful family in Boston, Massachusetts, Henry Cabot Lodge served in the Senate for more than thirty years. He took a leading role in many of the country's most important debates on foreign policy, including imperialism and the international role that the United States should play after World War I (1914–1918). Before entering politics, Lodge earned a Ph.D. at Harvard University in Massachusetts, and he wrote several books on American history.

In Their Own Words

In September 1898, Albert Beveridge was running for the U.S. Senate. Here is part of a campaign speech that he gave arguing that the United States should keep the Philippines.

[The Spanish-American War was] a war for civilization, a war for permanent peace, a war which, under God, although we knew it not, swung open to the republic the [doors] of the commerce of the world.... Fellow Americans, we are God's chosen people.... We cannot fly from our world duties...we cannot retreat from any soil where Providence has unfurled our banner; it is ours to save that soil for liberty and civilization.

Against War and Imperialism

Various groups of Americans opposed the Spanish-American War and the building of an American empire. Before the war, the anti-imperialists argued that the country should use diplomacy to end the violence in Spain. Anti-imperialists such as former senator Carl Schurz argued that the United States did not have to go to war with Spain to defend American honor. In truth, Schurz wrote, the United States was much stronger than Spain, so if the Americans defeated it in a war, "there would be little glory in our triumph."

Fast Fact

Along with Carl Schurz, leading anti-imperialists included business leader Andrew Carnegie, author Mark Twain, former U.S. president Benjamin Harrison, and social reformer Jane Addams.

The anti-imperialist forces had various reasons for not wanting overseas colonies, such as Cuba, Puerto Rico, and the Philippines. Running an empire would raise the risk of future conflicts between the United States and European powers over events and trade in Asia. That issue raised another concern among some anti-imperialists. They feared that the United States would have to spend more money on its military to defend its new empire. Those expenses would raise taxes. Even before the Spanish-American War, Theodore Roosevelt and other imperialists had called for a larger navy. Building an empire would require even more ships. Running an empire would also require a larger government bureaucracy. Many anti-imperialists did not want to increase the size of the federal government or give it more power.

Like the imperialists, some anti-imperialists used racial thinking to explain their positions. Their concerns were especially targeted at the Philippines. Filipinos, these anti-imperialists claimed, were not equal to white Americans and could never function in a democratic system. The United States would be better off not having anything to do with them.

On the other hand, some anti-imperialists opposed the racist thinking that they saw at the heart of the effort to build a U.S. empire. The imperialists assumed that they should run the Filipino society because they knew what was best for the Filipinos. Some anti-imperialists had actively opposed slavery in the United States. To them, imperialism would be similar to slavery for the people who lived under American colonial rule. Creating a new system like slavery, the anti-imperialists argued, went against the American ideals of freedom and liberty.

The anti-imperialists lost the debate over creating an American empire. The Philippines remained a U.S. colony until 1946. Guam and Puerto Rico are still U.S. possessions, though the local people have some control over their governments.

AN IMPERIAL WAR

When the Spanish-American War began, Filipinos were rebelling against Spain, trying to win their independence. Their leader, Emilio Aguinaldo, took control of a new Filipino government in January 1899, but the United States refused to recognize it or Filipino independence. Within a month, the Filipinos were once again fighting to control their own country—this time against U.S. troops. This war lasted until 1902, when the Americans ended the rebellion, though some fighting went on for several more years. More than 4,000 U.S. troops and 200,000 Filipinos—rebels and civilians—died during the war. The anti-imperialists saw this war as another example of the problems involved in running an empire and denying foreign peoples the chance to develop their own governments.

In Their Own Words

Here is part of an article that Carl Schurz wrote in 1898 opposing the U.S. attempt to take over Spanish lands.

[The companies] formed for distant adventure will be the most dangerous of all. Never having enough, their greed constantly grasping for more, they will seek to drive this country into new opportunities of conquest.... And the more such enterprises there are, the greater will be the danger of new wars, with all their demoralizing effects upon our democratic government.

CHAPTER SEVEN

The Industrial Policies of Henry Ford

WHAT

*Automaker Henry Ford introduces mass production
and the five-dollar-a-day salary.*

ISSUES

New demands on workers and the need for higher salaries

WHERE

Detroit, Michigan

WHEN

1913–1914

*D*uring the 1880s, inventors in Europe and the United States built the world's first automobiles. Some ran on steam power, others used batteries, and still others used the internal combustion engine, which ran on gasoline. Gas-powered cars became common, because the internal combustion engine was both powerful and easy to use, compared to the other two power sources.

In the United States, Detroit, Michigan, emerged as one of the early centers of the American auto industry. One of the pioneers there was Henry Ford. In 1903, he launched the Ford Motor Company. His goal was to give Americans a car that was lightweight, easy to operate and repair, and cheap enough for most people to buy. Describing his cars, Ford declared, "No man making a good salary will be unable to own one."

By 1908, Ford had perfected his ideal car, which he called the Model T. Ford decided to make and sell just this one type of car. Then he would not have to spend extra money to manufacture a wide variety of parts for different cars. Saving that money would keep his costs down, which would help make the Model T the cheapest car on the market.

Fast Fact

The Ford Motor Company's first car was called the Model A. Each new model was named after a different letter of the alphabet. After the success of the Model T, the company introduced a new Model A in 1927, and later gave its cars names, as other automakers did.

Henry Ford demonstrates one of his first cars. He established the Ford Motor Company in 1903.

HENRY FORD
(1863–1947)

As a teenager, Henry Ford decided that he wanted to make his own self-propelled vehicles. In 1896, he tested his first gas-powered car. After designing several successful racecars, Ford concentrated on building a car for the average American.

The success of his Model T made Ford one of the richest and best-known Americans of his day. Hailed as a business leader and inventor, Ford was sometimes criticized for his personal beliefs and his company's actions. A newspaper that he owned published articles that attacked Jews, and his company sometimes used violence against workers seeking better conditions. Despite his flaws, Ford is considered one of the most influential Americans of the twentieth century.

The Rise of Mass Production

Ford's company grew quickly to meet the demand for his new car. In 1908, he had about 450 workers in his plant. By 1913, the Ford Motor Company had more than 14,000 employees. Ford had trouble finding enough skilled workers to make his cars. He needed a building method that would let him make more cars with fewer workers and with workers who had not previously run the machines used to make metal parts.

To solve his problem, Ford took several different methods used before in industry, combined them, and created what is now known as mass production. The first step was using interchangeable parts to assemble the different pieces of a car. An engine, for example, included pistons—round, metal pieces that move up and down as the engine runs. Making all pistons interchangeable, or identical to each other, meant that any piston could be used in any engine. If a piston broke, any other piston could be used to replace it.

The idea of using interchangeable parts emerged in the late eighteenth century in France. The French government wanted its rifles made with identical parts to speed up production and repairs. At the time, however, the parts used to construct rifles and other items were made mostly by hand. Workers had a hard time ensuring that each part was identical to the next. The development of new machines to make identical parts made interchangeability a reality. During the nineteenth century, U.S. inventors developed many of these machines.

Ford also used assembly lines to move parts of the Model T through his plant. Ford said that he was inspired by meatpacking plants where animal carcasses moved through the plants on hooks attached to belts. The idea of moving items on mechanized belts also dated from the eighteenth century. U.S. inventor Oliver Evans used waterwheels to power belts that carried grain through a mill. During the nineteenth century, some factories used steam engines to power such belts, which were called conveyors. By Ford's day, electric motors powered the conveyors and chains that moved items through his plant.

The last step in Ford's system was increasing the division of labor—the idea that each worker should do one small task in the manufacturing of a product. In the earliest days of auto making, one worker would build an entire engine. Later, several workers would build one engine, with each worker focusing on one part of the engine. Ford took the division of labor one step further. In his new system, a worker might simply tighten one bolt on one part used to build a section of the engine as that part moved by the worker on a conveyor. Ford carefully studied how much workers had to move to complete their tasks and how much time it took them. For each part of the production process, he and his engineers came up with a speed that let the workers build the most possible parts with the fewest movements.

THE AMERICAN SYSTEM

As in France, the U.S. government hoped interchangeable parts would improve the production of guns. By the 1820s, several American companies were producing guns that used interchangeable parts. However, the process did not save as much money as the government had hoped. Still, the idea of interchangeable parts spread to other industries, and over time, the use of machines to make identical parts did reduce manufacturing costs. The British studied American production methods, which came to be called the American System. During the second half of the nineteenth century, this system was used to make such things as sewing machines, typewriters, farm equipment, and bicycles.

Shorter Day, Better Pay

As Ford was testing mass production, he also tried to improve the workers' morale. One of Ford's assistants studied morale and concluded that part of the solution was reducing the length of the workday and raising pay.

At the time, Ford's employees worked nine hours a day. In other industries, workers were on the job for ten hours or more. Ford's workers earned, on average, less than $2.50 a day. In October 1913, Ford set a minimum wage of $2.34 and raised wages for most workers. He followed this in January 1914 with a new plan to give workers five dollars a day—a salary that no factory worker in the world earned at that time. Ford also reduced the

Fast Fact

Ford tested his mass production system on an engine part called the flywheel magneto. In the past, one worker built this part in about twenty minutes. Using the assembly line and division of labor, a group of workers could build one in five minutes.

workday to eight hours and hired an extra 4,000 workers so that he could run his plant twenty-four hours a day.

The extra pay was actually part of a profit-sharing plan. Workers did not receive the money as part of their daily wage. Instead, they earned it if the company made a profit—and if they qualified. Ford placed some limits on who received the bonus, such as age and behavior outside of work.

Ford introduced the profit-sharing plan for several reasons. He believed that it would reduce worker turnover, the problem of workers taking a job with the company but soon leaving. "We wanted to pay these wages," he later wrote, "so that the business would be on a lasting foundation." The profit-sharing plan also served as a good form of advertising for Ford and the company. Before 1914, newspapers and magazines rarely wrote about Ford. After that year, he was the world's most famous industrial owner.

RIOT OVER WAGES

As soon as the Ford Motor Company announced its new pay plan, thousands of people flocked to Detroit looking for jobs. They stayed in the city even after the company said that it did not have new jobs at the moment. To clear the streets of the job seekers, the Detroit police turned fire hoses on them. Some of the unemployed then hurled rocks at the Ford plant's windows. A few protesters were arrested, and the rest finally left the plant.

Praising Ford's Ideas

Ford and his assistants saw immediately that mass production would let the company make more cars at a faster pace. Assembling the chassis, the main body of the car, took about two hours using the new methods, compared to about twelve hours the old way. Soon, Ford used mass production techniques to build a complete car.

The new system also let Ford hire unskilled workers—mostly immigrants. In the past, the company had to search for skilled workers or teach new methods to people who knew how to do a job a certain way—but not the way that Ford did it. His shop managers liked the idea of hiring unskilled workers and quickly teaching them what to do on the assembly lines. Ford thought that the workers welcomed doing one simple task over and over, since they did not have to make much effort to do their jobs.

The benefits of the five-dollar-a-day wage were just as obvious to Ford as were those of his new assembly lines. Before 1914, the Ford Motor Company had to hire 53,000 people a year to keep its total workforce at 14,000. The year after putting the new wage plan in place, the company only had to hire about 6,500 people. Most of them filled new jobs instead of replacing workers who had quit. The higher salary increased worker loyalty and improved the lives of workers. Ford said that he wanted to let his workers "[share] in our good fortune."

> **Fast Fact**
>
> In 1908, Ford sold about 6,000 Model Ts at $850 each. In 1916, the price had fallen to $360, and Ford sold more than 500,000 of the cars.

Some people outside the Ford Motor Company also welcomed the higher wage. Workers hoped that Ford's plan would force other companies to match his salaries if they wanted to attract new workers. Several ministers and social reformers also hoped that Ford's move would lead other companies to raise wages. Most industrial workers had faced low pay and difficult working conditions for centuries. Their children often had to work in order to help support their families. One minister said that the plan was "a particular answer to the world's cry for social justice."

In Their Own Words

In his 1922 autobiography (actually written by Samuel Crowther), Henry Ford expressed his ideas on the five-dollar-a-day wage. Here is part of what he wrote.

If we can distribute high wages, then that money is going to be spent and it will serve to make storekeepers and distributors and manufacturers and workers in other lines more prosperous and their prosperity will be reflected in our sales. Country-wide high wages spell country-wide prosperity.... Our profits...show that paying good wages is the most profitable way of doing business.

In 1914, the year this photograph of workers assembling engines for the Model T was taken, Henry Ford increased the pay for his employees on the assembly line.

Ford's Critics
and Their Arguments

Mass production increased Ford's profits, which led to the higher wages that he began offering in 1914. For individual workers, however, the new system led to new demands. Ford and his assistants carefully timed how long certain tasks should take, and the workers were expected to complete a certain number of parts in a day. If one worker slowed down, the whole assembly was affected. Workers had to work at a set pace, which some felt was faster than they could handle. One shop manager at the plant said that the one phrase he had to learn in many languages—since Ford hired so many immigrants—was "Hurry up." In 1914, the wife of one worker wrote to Ford that his new system drained her husband, who came home too tired to eat.

Some workers felt that their jobs under mass production were boring. Instead of making a product from start to finish, they simply performed a few tasks over and over. In 1917, one worker wrote that skilled workers "get little or no chance to use their skill."

Some workers also had complaints about the new wages. To get their five dollars a day, the workers had to let Ford and his company play a larger role in their private lives. Ford had investigators study the workers' personal habits and home lives. Workers who kept a clean home, did not gamble or drink, and saved their money were chosen for the profit-sharing. Workers with bad habits had to change their ways if they wanted the extra money. William Klann, a foreman at the plant, said that the men who worked for him "felt [the investigators] were interfering in their private lives."

The strongest arguments against higher wages came from other business owners and newspapers that supported their interests. Most complained that Ford's raise would put too much pressure on other industries to raise their wages. If they did not match Ford's salaries, these other companies might have trouble finding enough workers. Employees might also begin to demand even higher wages and other benefits. The *Wall Street Journal*, a New York newspaper, accused Ford of deliberately trying to force another Detroit carmaker out of business. A business organization in Detroit accused Ford of trying to destroy capitalism, the economic system of the United States.

However, mass production was found to help other companies increase their production while lowering costs. These companies began to offer higher salaries, as well. Paying workers more helped them buy the increased number of goods that were now being made under a mass production system.

In Their Own Words

Here is part of an article in the *Wall Street Journal* attacking Ford's five-dollar-a-day plan.

...to inject ten millions [of dollars] into a company's factory, and to double the minimum wage, without regard to length of service, is to apply Biblical or spiritual principles into a field where they do not belong.... If the newspapers of the day are correctly reporting the latest invention...of Henry Ford, he has in his social endeavor committed economic blunders, if not crimes. They may return to plague him and the industry he represents, as well as organized society.

CHAPTER EIGHT

The Coming of World War I

WHAT
The United States is pulled into World War I.

ISSUES
The desire to remain neutral; the need for the United States to
protect its interests and spread democracy

WHERE
Nationwide

WHEN
1914–1918

*I*n the early years of the twentieth century, U.S. foreign affairs focused mainly on Latin America and China. Those regions were seen as suppliers of natural resources and markets for U.S. products. Latin America drew extra attention, because it was closer to the United States. U.S. policy under the Monroe Doctrine, which had been issued by President James Monroe in 1823, stated that the country would limit European influence in the region. Several U.S. presidents sent troops to Latin American nations or islands in the Caribbean Sea when political problems seemed to threaten U.S. business interests. In the early 1900s, the United States built the Panama Canal, creating a shortcut through Panama that linked the Atlantic and Pacific Oceans.

While the United States was protecting and expanding its international business interests, a political assassination in Europe led the way to war. At the time, the continent's major nations were politically connected in two major groups, or alliances. On one side was the Triple Entente of Great Britain, France, and Russia. On the other was the Triple Alliance, or Central Powers, of Germany, Austria-Hungary, and the Ottoman Empire (now Turkey). Some of the members of these groups also had ties to other countries. Russia, for example, was friendly with Serbia.

Austria-Hungary, a Central European empire, ruled Bosnia. In neighboring Serbia, an independent country, some radical groups wanted to add Bosnia to their territory. In June 1914, a Serbian radical killed Archduke Franz Ferdinand, a member of the Austrian royal family. The assassination of the archduke created tension between Austria-Hungary and Serbia. Russia pledged to support the Serbs if a war broke out with Austria-Hungary. France and Great Britain would be allied with Russia, while Austria-Hungary would receive help from its allies. When Austria-Hungary and Serbia could not settle their dispute with diplomacy, they and their allies began what was known as the Great War. Today, the war is called World War I (1914–1918).

The American Response

As World War I began, the Central Powers took the early advantage, with German troops marching through Belgium and deep into France. Within a few months, however, the German advance stalled, while Russia fought the Central Powers in Eastern Europe.

The war stirred strong emotions among immigrants who had recently left their homelands and settled in America. Immigrants from the countries that formed the two sides tended to support their native lands in the war. President Woodrow Wilson called on all Americans to remain neutral, and he made neutrality the official U.S. policy. Wilson told the country, "Every man who really loves America will act and speak in the true spirit of neutrality, which is the spirit of...fairness and friendliness to all concerned."

Even though most Americans opposed taking an active role in the war, the United States took steps to expand its military. The country started a program called "preparedness." America, Wilson and others believed, should seek peace in Europe and stay out of the war but be prepared to fight in the future. Former president Theodore Roosevelt supported the preparedness effort. Soon after the war began, he said that the country should "speak softly and carry a big stick."

> *Fast Fact*
>
> As part of the preparedness campaign, Woodrow Wilson asked Congress to pay for 10 battleships and 100 submarines.

America Enters the War

The Atlantic Ocean became a dangerous place, as both Germany and Great Britain tried to disrupt their enemies' trade with the United States and other neutral countries. For the first time ever, nations used submarines during war. Germany called its subs U-boats, and they destroyed many ships—including British ships carrying American passengers. By January 1917, Germany announced that it would attack all ships, including

Fast Fact

In March 1916, Pancho Villa raided New Mexico, killing seventeen Americans. The violence led President Wilson to send U.S. troops after Villa.

neutral ones, that sailed in British waters. This tactic threatened the safety of U.S. ships.

Germany was increasingly worried about the Americans entering the war on the side of the Triple Entente (known during the war as the Allies). Therefore, the Germans tried to influence events in Mexico, where the United States had sent troops in 1916. The Americans were trying to hunt down Pancho Villa, a rebel seeking to control the Mexican government. The Germans encouraged Villa to fight the Americans, hoping that would keep the United States out of World War I.

Germany also dealt with the Mexican government. A German diplomat, Arthur Zimmerman, sent a telegram to the German ambassador in Mexico telling him that Germany wanted a formal alliance with Mexico. Once Germany won the war in Europe, the Germans would guarantee that Mexico received all the lands that the United States had taken from it after the Mexican War (1846–1848). British spies learned of the Zimmerman telegram and informed Wilson. The telegram, along with the German submarine warfare, convinced Wilson that Germany was a threat that he could not ignore. In April 1917, he asked Congress to declare war on Germany. Wilson said, "The world must be made safe for democracy.... The day has come when America is privileged to spend her blood and her might for the principles that gave her birth and happiness."

Fast Fact

About 2 million U.S. troops served overseas during World War I. About 112,000 Americans died—more than half from disease.

Despite the preparedness program, the United States had only about 200,000 troops when it entered World War I. By the end of the war, however, the country had more than 4 million troops. A little more than half were drafted—the government required them to serve. The rest were volunteers.

The first U.S. troops reached France in June 1917. Their commander was General John "Black Jack" Pershing. He insisted that the Americans should fight as separate units, not mixed in with French and British forces. The U.S. troops, however, relied on the other Allies for heavy weapons and transportation. The Americans helped the Triple Entente defeat the Germans, the main military power of the Triple Alliance. The war ended on November 11, 1918.

Gral. Obregon   Francisco Villa   Gral. Pershing

Famous Figures

JOHN PERSHING
(1860–1948)

During World War I, John Pershing above right, was the commander of the American Expeditionary Forces—the U.S. troops sent to Europe. Pershing had graduated from the U.S. Military Academy at West Point, New York, in 1886. His first fighting came in the West, against Native Americans. Pershing earned his nickname of "Black Jack" because he briefly commanded African American troops. At the time, black and white soldiers did not fight in the same units. Pershing fought in the Spanish-American War (1898) and then served in the Philippines after the United States took control of those islands. After World War I, Pershing served as the army chief of staff and worked to strengthen U.S. defenses.

In Favor of the Allies, Preparedness, and the War

Before the United States entered World War I, President Wilson wanted the country to remain neutral. In 1916, as he campaigned for a second term as president, Wilson used the slogan "He kept us out of war." Still, he believed that the United States should not cut itself off from Europe but continue to trade with both sides and use its influence to end the war.

Some Americans, however, clearly favored the Triple Entente, because of U.S. business and cultural ties with the British. Many Americans were also suspicious of the Germans, who were ruled by a dictator, Kaiser Wilhelm II. He and his country seemed intent on spreading their influence around the world. The Germans angered many Americans when they attacked Belgium, a neutral nation, and killed civilians in the process. The sinking of the *Lusitania,* a British passenger ship with Americans on board, also stirred hatred of Germany.

In private, Wilson also leaned toward the British and against the Germans, and some of his public actions reflected this. Before the United States entered the war, Wilson approved almost $3 billion in loans to the Allies, while Germany received just $27 million. Wilson also tended to overlook British efforts that hurt American trade with the Central Powers.

Many of the Americans who supported the British also backed the preparedness effort. Others, including some military leaders, believed that preparedness was the only way to remain neutral. If the United States had a strong military, other countries would not threaten its interests. Of course, a larger military would also help the country if it did enter World War I at a later date.

The preparedness movement was popular with average Americans, as well as military and political leaders. In 1916, parades in a dozen cities drew more than 500,000 people calling for the country to improve its defenses and prepare for war. Supporters saw military service as a way to make immigrants more accepted and acceptable in American culture and generally strengthen U.S. youth. One Chicago, Illinois, newspaper said that compulsory military service would "reduce the criminal rate, produce a higher type of manhood, and level class distinction."

After Congress finally declared war in April 1917, William Howard Taft was just one of the prominent Americans who supported it. In a speech that June, the former U.S. president acknowledged that some Americans believed that the country should have entered the war earlier. Still, the delay showed that United States was not eager to fight. America chose war only when "the situation has been such that no self-respecting nation...could avoid doing what we are doing."

THE *LUSITANIA*

On May 1, 1915, the British passenger ship *Lusitania* sailed from New York, heading to England. The ship carried almost 2,000 people, including 197 Americans. The *Lusitania* also carried food and weapons for the British war effort against Germany. The Germans had warned Americans not to sail on British ships. The Germans considered them possible targets, since the British used passenger ships to carry military supplies. On May 7, off the coast of Ireland, a German U-boat fired a torpedo that sank the *Lusitania*. Of the Americans on board, 128 died, and a total of 1,128 lives were lost. Germany believed that it had acted legally, since the ship was in a war zone. Wilson protested the attack to Germany, but he and most Americans were still not ready to go to war.

When World War I began, Professor Robert Herrick was a pacifist—someone who opposes all violence and wars. After visiting France, however, he changed his views about the need to fight the Germans. Here is part of an article he wrote for a U.S. magazine.

I know that many Americans are still unable to determine for themselves that any extraordinary issue is at stake in Europe today.... But even the...simplest workman in France is eternally assured that he is fighting...the battle of the whole world in defense of its best ideals, its best traditions.

Against Preparedness and the War

While many Americans at first supported neutrality in 1914, a core group believed that any war was wrong. Other people opposed the war for specific reasons. Some supported socialism, an economic system that calls for the government rather than private businesses to own factories and control the economy. The socialists believed that the war was being fought to make money for private business owners, while poor people did the actual fighting—and dying. Socialists also believed that workers should remain loyal to their class—other workers, no matter where they lived—and not their countries. Some nonsocialists shared the view that the war made profits for businesses while ignoring its effects on soldiers and average citizens.

A much larger group of Americans opposed the preparedness movement. Many of them were progressives—largely well-educated people who wanted to reform American politics and society. Progressives wanted to use the government to tackle such problems as homelessness and poverty. They also wanted to end corruption in government and limit the power of big businesses. Many progressives did not want the United States to spend money on defense when the money could be better used for reform efforts. Jane Addams was a leading progressive. When Wilson called for building more ships, she asked, "Why spend $45,000,000 for warships, when they will only be reduced to [the] scrap heap after this war?"

Some progressives in Congress truly opposed the war; others came from areas where many German Americans lived, and these voters tended to oppose Great Britain in the war. Robert La Follette, a progressive from Wisconsin, was one U.S. senator who accused the U.S. government of favoring the British and failing to be truly neutral. That policy, he and others believed, had led to the increased German attacks on U.S. ships.

Some people continued to oppose the war after the United States entered it. President Wilson asked Congress to pass laws that limited public criticism of the war, the government, and the military. Most Americans accepted these new restrictions. They felt that the country had to be united to win the war.

In Their Own Words

Oswald Garrison Villard, a New York newspaper publisher, spoke out often against preparedness and the possible U.S. entry into the war. Here is part of an article that he wrote in 1916.

American sanity and intelligence will speedily see that the outcry [for] more soldiers and ships comes not from the masses of the people, but from the fortunate classes in life.... There is no slavery in the world like this to arms, none that today so checks the growth of liberty, of democracy....

CHAPTER NINE

The League of Nations

VERSAILLES.

1919

LEAGUE OF NATIONS

WHAT
*President Woodrow Wilson promotes
an international organization.*

ISSUE
U.S. membership in the League of Nations

WHERE
Nationwide

WHEN
1919–1920

zen.]

[Brooklyn, U.S.

An Expected Arrival.

Will the stork make good as to this infant?

*I*n April 1917, President Woodrow Wilson told Americans that the United States was entering World War I (1914–1918) "to make the world safe for democracy." Two groups of European nations, the Triple Entente (the Allies) and the Triple Alliance (the Central Powers), had been fighting each other since 1914. Most Americans, including Wilson, had wanted to keep the United States out of the war, but many Americans were also sympathetic to the British and the French, the two major forces in the Triple Entente. Germany, the leader of the Central Powers, stirred American hatred with its brutal attack against Belgium and its submarine warfare against merchant and passenger ships.

Wilson and other Americans distrusted and disliked Germany and the other Central Powers for another reason. These nations had kings or other rulers who limited political freedoms. Defeating them would give Wilson and the Allies the chance to spread democracy in those lands and in the territories that they controlled. When World War I ended in November 1918, Wilson planned to play a large role in shaping the postwar world.

The Fourteen Points

In January 1918, Wilson outlined for Congress the fourteen key issues, or points, that he wanted the Allies to address at the end of the war. Although the fighting would last for most of the year, the Allies assumed at this time that they would win the war.

In his "Fourteen Points" speech, Wilson stressed that all future diplomacy should be done in the open, with no secret treaties between nations. Wilson wanted the European nations to reduce the size of their militaries, and he called for all troops to leave territory that they had invaded during the war. Wilson's last point called for "a general association of nations" that would guarantee "political independence and territorial integrity to great and small states alike." This association was later called the League of Nations.

After the Allies' victory, Wilson left for Paris, France, to work on the peace treaty between the two sides. At the peace meetings, he had some disagreements with British and French leaders. They wanted Germany to pay reparations—money that would pay for some of the Allied losses. The British and French also wanted Germany to give up some of its territory and severely reduce the size of its military. Other Allies, such as Italy and Japan, also hoped to gain territory from the defeated Central Powers. Although Wilson's Fourteen Points called for a general reduction in the size of armies and the breaking up of the Central Powers, the other Allies wanted to go much further as a form of punishment.

In the end, the peace treaty gave the British and French much of what they wanted. Wilson accepted the final treaty, called the Treaty of Versailles, because he wanted British and French support for the League of Nations. To him, having an organization that could prevent future wars was the most important part of the peace process. Wilson hoped that the League would become the "moral force of the world" that would keep the peace that came with the Allies' victory.

The Structure of the League

The U.S. representatives in France, led by Wilson, worked with Allied diplomats to draft the covenant, or basic agreement, that created the League of Nations. The final covenant had twenty-six articles. The League had an assembly, which included representatives from all member nations. A smaller council had permanent members from five Allied nations: the United States, Great Britain, France, Italy, and Japan. Four other nations, selected by the assembly, would also sit on this council for varying terms decided by the assembly.

The main articles of the covenant touched on Wilson's primary concerns: preserving the peace reached in Paris and preventing future wars. Article Eight called for limits on the number of weapons that each country built. Article Ten said that League members would help each other if they faced a threat to their independence or if an enemy claimed their territory. The League was also supposed to settle problems that arose between any member nations. Still, although the League of Nations was focused on peace, the agreement under the covenant called for the use of military force, when necessary, to punish nations who broke it.

In February 1919, Wilson introduced the covenant to the other delegates at the peace talks. The covenant for the League of Nations became the first part of the Treaty of Versailles, which Germany signed on June 28, 1919.

President Woodrow Wilson announces the end of World War I to Congress on November 11, 1918. Ten months earlier he had outlined his peace plan, also known as the Fourteen Points. The last of the points involved the establishment of "a general association of nations," which would become the League of Nations.

The Battle for the League

When he arrived home, Wilson faced difficulties with the U.S. Senate over the League of Nations. Under the Constitution, two-thirds of the Senate must ratify a treaty before it can go into effect. The Republican Party controlled the Senate, and Wilson, a Democrat, was not ready to compromise with Republican senators on the League and the role that he thought the United States should play in international affairs.

At the time, the U.S. Senate was split into three groups regarding the League of Nations. Most Democrats—members of Wilson's party—supported the League. An equally large group of about forty senators wanted reservations, or extra wording in the treaty that would protect U.S. interests. These senators were called Reservationists and included some Democrats, though most were Republicans. A much smaller group of senators, almost all Republican, opposed the League in any form. They were called the Irreconcilables.

Wilson could not win approval unless he convinced some of the Reservationists to accept the League. He gave in to a few of their demands and accepted some basic reservations, but he refused to make any major changes. Starting in September, he traveled across the country, trying to win popular support for his plan. If the public backed the League, some senators might vote for the treaty. In just three weeks, Wilson gave forty speeches promoting the treaty and the League. He won the support of more than half the country's governors and many state lawmakers, but leading senators continued to oppose him.

> *Fast Fact*
>
> The Reservationists were split into two distinct groups: Mild and Strong. The Mild Reservationists, a much smaller group with members from both parties, favored the League but wanted to address some of the issues raised by the Strong Reservationists.

The Vote and After

As the Senate continued to debate the treaty, Wilson suffered a stroke, a physical ailment that affects the brain. He could not move the left side of his body and was forced to stay in bed. Wilson could not continue his public fight for the League while his opponents continued to attack it.

Through October and most of November 1919, some senators tried to change the treaty or add reservations. On November 19, the debate finally ended and the Senate voted. First, it rejected the Reservationists' effort to add conditions for accepting the treaty. Then the Senate voted on accepting the treaty as it was written, without any changes. Thirty-seven Democrats and one Republican voted for the treaty—short of the sixty-one needed to ratify it.

These votes came on the last day of the Senate's session for the year. It did not meet again until March 1920. At that time, the Senate considered the treaty once more. Wilson, still sick but slightly better, had continued to oppose reservations. He wrote in January, "It is the more important not to create the impression that we are trying to escape obligations." Despite Wilson's position, the Senate voted on a proposal to ratify the treaty with reservations. Once again, the Senate rejected it.

Fast Fact

Since the Senate did not approve the Treaty of Versailles, Congress passed a joint resolution in 1921 declaring that the United States was no longer at war with Germany, Austria, or Hungary.

As the Senate was debating whether or not the United States should join the League of Nations, the League began operating in 1920 with the countries that had already agreed to join it. The League officially ended in 1946, when it was replaced with the United Nations (UN), which still exists today. After the last Senate vote on the League, a few U.S. politicians suggested that the country should reconsider joining it, but most Americans were content that their country never gained membership in the organization. Some historians, however, argue that Wilson was right about the need for the United States to join the League. Its presence might have helped solve some of the international problems that later led to World War II (1939–1945).

Arguments against the League

The forces against the League had various reasons for opposing it. The Irreconcilables tended to be isolationists—they did not want the United States to take part in any alliance or league that might force the country to enter a foreign war. The leading isolationists were Republican senators William Borah of Idaho and Hiram Johnson of California.

The League's covenant, isolationists believed, would also limit U.S. foreign policy as spelled out in the Monroe Doctrine, created by President James Monroe in 1823. The Monroe Doctrine said that the United States would take military action if any European nation tried to interfere with political events in North or South America. Wilson got around this criticism by changing the covenant before it was signed in Europe so that the United States would be free to act under the Monroe Doctrine without League interference.

Isolationists also saw the "Old World" of Europe as corrupt. Having closer ties with the European nations would weaken America's moral strength and its democratic government. Borah said that gaining the power to shape world events was not worth losing the country's democratic values. By acting alone, the United States could "continue her mission in the cause of peace, of freedom, and of civilization."

The Reservationists realized that the United States had a role to play in world affairs. However, like the isolationists, they worried that the League's covenant would force the United States to take actions—such as declaring war—that did not serve the country's interests. The leading Reservationist was Henry Cabot Lodge, a Republican senator from Massachusetts. The Reservationists wanted to protect Congress's power under the Constitution to declare war. Lodge also believed that the United States would hurt itself by "meddling and muddling in every quarrel...which affects the world." The nation had to be able to choose when to become involved in the world's problems.

Lodge proposed adding fourteen reservations to the covenant. Most specified that Congress would decide how the United States carried out its duties in the League. One reservation repeated the notion that the League could not limit U.S. actions under the Monroe Doctrine, while another stated that the League could not influence any U.S. laws that dealt with domestic issues.

Some of the League's opponents also thought that President Wilson had cut them out of the process that shaped the treaty and the League. Republican Warren Harding of Ohio, a future U.S. president, felt that Wilson deserved to lose on the treaty vote, because he had "negotiated it without admitting the existence of the Senate." Since the war, some senators thought that Wilson had tried to increase his own power at the expense of Congress. The League proposal seemed another example of this. Wilson's opponents also did not like the fact that Wilson had refused to compromise on the reservations.

In Their Own Words

Here is part of a speech that Henry Cabot Lodge made against the League of Nations.

I will go as far as anyone in world service, but the first step to world service is the maintenance of the United States....

You may call me selfish if you will...or use any other harsh adjective you see fit to apply, but an American I was born, an American I have remained all my life. I can never be anything else but an American, and I must think of the United States first, and when I think of the United States first in an arrangement like this I am thinking of what is best for the world, for if the United States fails, the best hopes of mankind fail with it.

Wilson Argues for the League

To Wilson, the League of Nations was the diplomatic tool for preserving peace among the world's largest nations. The United States, as a powerful country with strong morals, should play a leading role in the League. Wilson thought that most Americans would share his vision. Opponents, he said in June 1919, wanted to "turn back to those bad days of selfish contest."

At the start of the fight to ratify the Treaty of Versailles, Wilson said that any reservations might threaten the whole peace process. Changes would mean going back to Europe for approval by the other Allies, and they might then want to make their own changes. This argument lost power, however, after the British said that they would accept some reservations.

Wilson then spoke out against some of the specific reservations, especially the ones about the League members' agreement to use force, if necessary, to prevent a larger war. Wilson told Americans that without the League—and the United States in

On his way to Paris in December 1918 for the peace conference that would draft the Treaty of Versailles, President Wilson boards the ocean liner George Washington. For Wilson, the most important provision of the treaty was the establishment of the League of Nations. The League of Nations was established in 1920, but the United States never joined it.

it—the world would face another huge international conflict. He asserted that the language of the covenant did not mean that the country could be forced into a war. The United States, as a member of the permanent council, had to approve any joint military action, unless the country was already part of the dispute being considered. If the United States were part of the dispute, Wilson noted, "you are in the scrap anyhow." If the country were already in a dispute, it would be better off having the rest of the League on its side.

Wilson targeted other specific reservations, as well. The Senate did not need to address the Monroe Doctrine, since the changes already made in the covenant protected U.S. interests in South America. Wilson also said that the League would not affect U.S. laws, so the reservation on domestic issues was unnecessary. In general, however, the president did not make many specific points on the reservations or his critics' complaints. Wilson focused on the larger issue—the role that the United States should play in preserving peace.

In Their Own Words

Here is part of a speech that President Wilson gave in Omaha, Nebraska, during his national tour of 1919.

My fellow citizens, this is one of the great charters of human liberty, and the man who picks flaws in it...forgets...that the counsels of more than twenty nations combined [agreed to] the adoption of this great instrument.... For the first time in history the counsels of mankind are to be drawn together...for the purpose of defending the rights and improving the conditions of working people...all over the world. Such a thing as that was never dreamed of before.

CHAPTER TEN

Prohibition

WHAT

*Congress and the states pass the Eighteenth Amendment
to the U.S. Constitution, which prohibits the production
and sale of alcohol.*

ISSUE

*The social and political problems caused by alcohol
versus the personal freedom to drink*

WHERE

Nationwide

WHEN

1917–1933

Since colonial times, alcohol has been a part of daily life for many Americans. Early settlers made their own beer and hard—alcoholic—cider. Wealthy Americans bought wine and other alcoholic beverages made in Europe. Rum was an important American product during the eighteenth century, forming part of the overseas trade that brought African slaves to the colonies. Pennsylvania farmers made a type of whiskey from corn or rye, and in 1794, they protested a tax on their product. President George Washington led a military force that finally ended this "Whiskey Rebellion." At times, drinking alcohol was safer than drinking water. Into the nineteenth century, towns did not always have the technology to provide clean water to their citizens.

By the early nineteenth century, however, a movement developed to temper, or restrain, the drinking of alcohol. Social reformers reacted to the growing problems tied to alcohol abuse. Workers who drank during the day could not do their jobs well, and alcoholics tended to spend all their money on drink, leaving their families struggling to survive. Also, doctors and other educated people came to believe that alcohol could damage a person's health. Ministers, meanwhile, preached that alcohol came from the devil and that staying sober was the best way to remain true to God's teachings. The anti-alcohol forces formed temperance leagues, which encouraged people to stop drinking alcohol.

> **Fast Fact**
>
> In colonial times and the first years of independence, political candidates often served alcohol to potential voters to win their support. During one local election in Virginia, George Washington provided voters with more than 100 gallons (380 liters) of rum, beer, cider, and alcoholic punch.

From Temperance to Prohibition

The temperance movement sparked an effort to prohibit alcohol altogether. In 1851, Maine became the first state to prohibit its residents from making and selling alcohol. Several other states followed, but Maine was the only one of these states to keep its anti-alcohol laws in place through the nineteenth century. In 1869, a Prohibition Party formed, pledging to ban alcohol with a constitutional amendment. Other anti-alcohol groups included the Women's Christian Temperance Union (WCTU), founded in 1874, and the Anti-Saloon League (ASL), which began in 1893.

The various anti-alcohol groups tended to have their greatest strength in rural parts of the country. Their members usually belonged to various Protestant churches that strictly enforced rules from the Bible. People who opposed alcohol associated it with large cities and the immigrants who lived there.

The Evangelical Church Army was one of many temperance groups that sprang up nationwide in the last half of the 1800s.

In the early twentieth century, the ASL became the most powerful prohibition group. The ASL worked across the country, hoping to change the laws regarding alcohol one state at a time. If it could not win total prohibition, the league tried to pass state and local laws that let individual towns or counties decide if they wanted to "go dry." With this "local option" strategy, the ASL and its allies put saloons out of business in large parts of the South.

The ASL also developed influence in Washington, D.C. Along with the WCTU, it convinced Congress to ban the sale of alcohol on military bases and restrict its use on Native American reservations. In 1913, the ASL worked with its friends in Congress to pass the Webb-Kenyon Act. This law made it a federal crime for anyone to bring alcohol into a state or territory that had

Fast Fact

People who supported prohibition were often called "drys," while people who wanted to allow drinking were called "wets."

prohibited its sale or manufacture. President William Howard Taft vetoed the law, but Congress used its constitutional power to override the veto and put Webb-Kenyon into effect. The new law marked the first time that the national government played a major part in the prohibition movement.

By the following year, about a dozen states had laws that totally prohibited the sale of alcohol. Representative Richmond Hobson of Alabama introduced a proposal in Congress to create a constitutional amendment that banned the sale and manufacture of alcohol, with only a few exceptions. However, Hobson's proposed amendment failed to win enough votes.

Fast Fact
Under the U.S. Constitution, two-thirds of the members of each house of Congress must approve a constitutional amendment. The amendment then must be approved by three-quarters of the states before it can take effect.

War and Prohibition

When World War I (1914–1918) began in Europe, Americans, for the most part, wanted to stay out of the war. At the same time, many public officials believed that the country should prepare for future wars by strengthening its military. The drive for "preparedness" carried over into personal habits, such as drinking. People who drank alcohol, the drys claimed, would not be alert and efficient enough to produce war supplies or train to become effective soldiers.

After April 1917, when the United States entered World War I, the U.S. government began to ration some foods and fuels so that it would have enough supplies to send to its European allies. Beer and many hard liquors are made from grains—one of the types of food that the government rationed. The drys said that reducing liquor consumption would aid the rationing effort.

With the country at war and with many drys in Congress, the ASL was able to have another prohibition amendment introduced in Congress. In December 1917, both houses of Congress passed the new amendment. A little more than a year later, thirty-six out of forty-eight states had approved the Eighteenth Amendment. National prohibition went into effect in January 1920. It was now illegal for anyone to make or sell alcohol or bring it into the country.

To enforce the new amendment, Congress passed the Volstead Act. This law defined an illegal beverage as anything with more than 0.5 percent alcohol in it. The Volstead Act also made exceptions for the use of alcohol, primarily for industries, doctors, scientists, and religious groups that used wine in their ceremonies. Wayne Wheeler, a lawyer for the ASL, played a large role in writing this law, though Congress made changes to his proposals. Still, Wheeler and the ASL were the driving force behind national prohibition.

> *Fast Fact*
> Eventually, forty-six states approved the Eighteenth Amendment. Only Rhode Island and Connecticut did not.

Famous Figures

WAYNE WHEELER
(1869–1927)

Wayne Wheeler joined the ASL in 1893 while attending Oberlin College in Ohio, and he worked for the organization for the rest of his life. His hatred of alcohol came from a personal experience. When Wheeler was a boy, a drunken neighbor had stabbed him with a pitchfork.

To help the ASL argue its positions in court, Wheeler became a lawyer. He eventually handled 2,000 law cases that dealt with prohibition issues. In 1919, he moved to Washington, D.C., to take the ASL's message to Congress, and he wrote the original version of the Volstead Act. By the time that the Eighteenth Amendment went into effect, Wheeler was America's best-known and most powerful dry.

The Effects of Prohibition

Although the drys had achieved their goal, the prohibition against alcohol never worked as well as they hoped it would. Congress did not spend enough money to enforce the Volstead Act, and some states ignored illegal activities within their borders. Many Americans ignored the law by making their own alcohol at home or buying it from bootleggers—people who illegally brought in alcohol from overseas or secretly made it in America.

The profits available from selling illegal liquor created a huge network of organized crime. Bootlegging sparked violence between the criminals and law officers trying to stop them. During the 1920s, an estimated 190 people, including 55 officers, were killed as a direct result of enforcing the Volstead Act.

Throughout the 1920s, wets argued that prohibition had created more problems than it solved. In 1932, the Democratic Party chose Franklin Roosevelt as its presidential candidate. The Democrats officially called for an end to prohibition. Roosevelt won the election, and in 1933, he convinced Congress to pass a law that legalized beer with 3.2 percent alcohol in it. The same year, Congress passed the Twenty-first Amendment, which repealed, or overturned, the Eighteenth Amendment. By the end of the year, thirty-six states had approved the Twenty-first Amendment, and national prohibition was over.

Fast Fact

Boat and ship captains who carried illegal alcohol into the United States were called "rum runners." One of the most famous was William McCoy. The expression "the real McCoy" comes from his smuggling quality liquor into the country.

The Arguments for Prohibition

The prohibitionists made many of the same arguments that had been made against alcohol since the early nineteenth century. Alcohol abuse led to accidents at work and violence in homes. A drunk father could not hold a job or care for his family.

Also, science had gathered more evidence that heavy drinking caused health problems. During World War I, an ASL poster said that between 1900 and 1908, 33,000 American men had died from alcoholism or liver disease caused by drinking.

Some of the arguments against alcohol were still based on the religious belief that liquor was associated with sin and the devil, while people who did not drink were carrying out God's will; if the country allowed any drinking at all, it risked losing God's blessing. As one prohibitionist newspaper put it, "The evil is a national evil.... God...accepts no action of isolated members as [reason to forgive] the nation's sin."

The ASL tried to shut down saloons and bars because, it said, some owners either allowed or ignored other illegal activities, such as gambling. Bar owners also tended to ignore laws regarding the hours they could stay open and the drinking age. Saloons seemed to promote a general attitude of breaking or ignoring the law. One religious leader called saloons "the deadliest enemy of the American home."

The saloons were not only a moral problem; they had a negative influence on politics, as well. In some cities, political leaders met in saloons, and sometimes, voters chose their candidates in them. People who wanted to reform politics thought that alcohol corrupted the election process. Voters could be bribed to vote a certain way with the promise of getting free drinks, or a person under the influence of alcohol could be persuaded to vote for a particular candidate. The profits that saloons made were also sometimes used to bribe local police and elected officials so that the saloon keepers could break the laws and not worry about being arrested or shut down. The profits from alcohol could also influence political decisions, as large breweries and distilleries made donations to national leaders.

Fast Fact

After the repeal of the Eighteenth Amendment, several states kept state laws prohibiting alcohol. Mississippi was the last state to end prohibition in 1966.

Opponents of prohibition parade in a car in 1923, making their message clear. Most opponents of the Eighteenth Amendment, which went into effect in 1920, based their objections on both individual and states' rights, namely, that the federal government had no right to infringe on either.

In Their Own Words

In 1914, Richmond Hobson spoke in favor of a prohibition amendment. The amendment did not pass Congress, but supporters of prohibition made similar arguments three years later, when the Eighteenth Amendment was approved.

Thus a man is little less of a man after each drink he takes. In this way continued drinking causes a progressive weakening of the will and a progressive growing of the craving, so that after a time, if persisted in, there must come a point where the will power can not control the craving and the victim is in the grip of the habit.

Arguments against Prohibition

A varied group of people and organizations spoke out against prohibition. They included immigrants who considered alcohol a normal part of everyday life. Germans, for example, considered beer a food—"liquid bread"—and Italians and others enjoyed wine with their meals. In many neighborhoods, saloons often functioned as important social centers where people could meet over a drink to exchange greetings and information.

Some saw the issue as one of individual liberty: The federal government did not have the right to tell people that they could not drink. Other opponents believed that the issue was states' rights: Each state should decide on its own if it wanted to limit or prohibit the sale of alcohol. States that wanted to restrict alcohol had already passed prohibition laws. As Senator Oscar Underwood of Alabama said, Congress had already given the states powers that "the most extreme prohibition advocate has demanded to enable the states to enforce their laws at home."

Opponents of prohibition predicted that if the states approved the Eighteenth Amendment, millions of Americans would find ways to break the law, especially since alcohol could be made at home or smuggled in from other countries. Some wealthy business owners feared that prohibition could raise their taxes. Before prohibition, the states and federal government taxed alcohol. If it were illegal, people would no longer have to pay the taxes, and the governments would tax other goods as a new source of money. In response, in 1919, the business owners formed the Association Against the Prohibition Amendment (AAPA).

Another economic argument came from the companies that made alcohol. These companies said that they would not make enough money producing other products and would have to go out of business.

Fast Fact

In 1880, the United States had about 150,000 saloons. Within twenty years, that number had doubled, despite the early successes of the ASL. Most of the growth took place in industrialized cities in the Northeast and Midwest.

Fast Fact

In June 1919, 10,000 union members held a rally in Washington, D.C., to protest the Eighteenth Amendment.

Labor unions—associations of workers that fight for better wages and working conditions—feared that some of their members would lose their jobs. Some labor leaders also claimed that workers would rebel against the government's stepping into their private lives by prohibiting them from drinking.

One official at an auto company said, "The great mass of our workmen...feel that prohibition...is a scheme to deny them something which their more fortunate brothers with money can have almost at will." The wealthy, the workers thought, could afford the high prices that bootleggers would charge. Working people, however, would have a harder time getting around the law.

Eventually, the crime and violence that went along with bootlegging convinced Americans to end prohibition. Bad economic times also played a role. In October 1929, the stock market crashed, and many people lost money. Soon after, the country's economy sharply weakened, creating the Great Depression. Millions of Americans lost their homes and their jobs. Ending prohibition meant that breweries and other companies could hire workers and that both the state and federal government could once again collect taxes on alcohol. The money could then be used to help people suffering from the effects of the Great Depression.

In Their Own Words

The AAPA could not keep the Eighteenth Amendment out of the Constitution, but throughout the 1920s, the group argued for its repeal. Here is a selection from an AAPA document against prohibition.

Our Constitutional guarantees...have been violated. [National prohibition] grants and withholds privileges upon a difference of religious belief. The right to govern ourselves in local affairs—a right won by our ancestors in three generations of struggle—is ignored.

CHAPTER ELEVEN

The Nineteenth Amendment

WHAT
Congress and the states pass an amendment to the
U.S. Constitution that gives women the right to vote.

ISSUE
The role that women should play in politics and society

WHERE
Nationwide

WHEN
1918-1920

*D*uring the nineteenth century, some American women became involved with abolitionism, the effort to end slavery in the United States. The most active of these female abolitionists often confronted men who did not think that women should play a role in social or political affairs. Facing unequal treatment, such women as Lucretia Mott and Elizabeth Cady Stanton helped start the first women's movement in the United States. Their goal was equal rights for women in all aspects of life.

In 1848, Mott, Stanton, and their supporters held a convention in Seneca Falls, New York. Stanton wrote a "Declaration of Rights and Sentiments." She modeled this on the Declaration of Independence, which Thomas Jefferson wrote in 1776, when the American colonies declared their independence from Great Britain. To Stanton, the most important right that women deserved was suffrage, or the right to vote. Many men, however—and some women—rejected the idea that women should be allowed to vote. Only men, many Americans believed, had the skills to carry out government policies and choose leaders, and state voting laws did not include women.

Fast Fact
At first, NWSA did not accept men as members. AWSA was cofounded by a man and did accept male members.

For the rest of her life, Stanton worked on many issues relating to women's roles and rights in society, but suffrage remained one of her main concerns. Helping her in the fight was Susan B. Anthony. In 1869, the two women founded the National Woman Suffrage Association (NWSA) to address voting rights and other women's issues. Later that year, another group, the American Woman Suffrage Association (AWSA), was formed, focusing solely on suffrage. The women who joined these and similar groups were known as suffragists or suffragettes.

ARRESTED FOR VOTING

During the early 1870s, some women illegally voted in political elections to protest their lack of equal rights. They believed that the Fourteenth and Fifteenth Amendments gave all U.S. citizens the right to vote. These amendments were passed after the Civil War (1861–1865) to give freed slaves political rights. However, the Fourteenth Amendment specifically mentioned only male voters. In 1872, Susan B. Anthony was arrested after she voted in the presidential election. At Anthony's trial, the judge refused to use a jury and found her guilty himself, then fined her $100. Anthony refused to pay the fine.

Success and Setbacks

While Stanton, Anthony, and others worked for women's suffrage on a national level, some western territories acted on their own. In 1869, the territory of Wyoming gave women the right to vote, as well as to sit on juries and hold public office. Wyoming had only about 9,000 people at the time, most of them men, and the lawmakers thought that granting suffrage would bring women to the territory. Anthony told women that they should "emigrate to Wyoming and make a model State of it by sending a woman Senator to the National Capital." The next year, Utah followed suit, and both territories kept suffrage for women when they joined the Union as states in the 1890s.

By 1900, women across the country had made some progress in winning the rights called for at the Seneca Falls Convention. Tens of thousands of women attended college, and all women had more opportunities to work outside the home. Most states, however, still considered fathers to be the sole legal guardians of a family's children, and despite the gains in the West, most women could not vote.

> *Fast Fact*
>
> Before 1900, Colorado and Idaho joined Wyoming and Utah in granting female suffrage.

The two main suffragist groups, NWSA and AWSA, united in 1890 to create the National American Woman Suffrage Association (NAWSA). Other women's organizations also joined the suffragists' struggle. The Women's Christian Temperance Union (WCTU), which opposed alcohol, also supported suffrage. Both the anti-alcohol movement and suffrage were two main political issues of the progressive era. During this time, many educated Americans of both sexes and all major political parties wanted to improve social and economic conditions for workers, farmers, women, and immigrants.

Many African American women also joined the suffragist movement. With the right to vote, they believed, they could help their entire race and women, as well. Some white suffragist leaders, however, were concerned with winning suffrage for white women, not all women. This feeling reflected the reality of racism, especially in the South. White males would be more likely to welcome white women as voters than to accept black female voters.

ATTACKING IMMIGRANTS

Racism was not the only negative tactic that emerged in the suffragist movement. Some of the leaders also appealed to nativism, the idea that immigrants were not equal to American-born white citizens. Some native-born Americans especially disliked immigrants who were Catholic or Jewish. During the late nineteenth and early twentieth centuries, most political and social leaders in the United States were Protestant, as were most leaders of the suffragist movement. These women argued that if uneducated immigrant men, especially Catholics and Jews, could vote, how could the country deny suffrage to educated, native-born Protestant women? The suffragists, hoping to win the support of male nativists, did not try to include women immigrants in their groups.

Seeking a National Amendment

Until 1910, the number of states that allowed suffrage remained at four. The next decade, however, saw twenty-three states grant women's suffrage. The movement also began to focus on adding a constitutional amendment that would guarantee women the right to vote across the country. Carrie Chapman Catt was president of NAWSA for many years. In 1910, she told members of Congress that they should consider such an amendment, if they were "believer[s] in democracy and individual liberty."

> *Fast Fact*
> Between 1906 and 1910, membership in NAWSA increased from about 12,000 to 117,000.

In 1907, a new organization joined the effort for women's suffrage. Harriet Stanton Blatch, daughter of Elizabeth Cady Stanton, helped found the Equality League of Self-Supporting Women. It soon changed its name to the Women's Political Union (WPU). Blatch wanted women to be even more vocal in demanding their rights. In 1910, the WPU organized the first major suffrage parade, in New York City. Suffrage parades and rallies then spread to other cities, where many women had a chance to take part.

The National Woman's Party

One memorable suffrage parade took place in 1913, during the inauguration of President Woodrow Wilson. Alice Paul, a member of NAWSA, wanted to bring more attention to the suffrage amendment. She told women in the states that had suffrage to vote against the parties in power if they refused to support suffrage. Wilson, a Democrat, was the first U.S. president to face this tactic. Paul and her supporters urged western women to vote for any party other than the Democrats.

In 1917, Paul helped found the National Woman's Party (NWP). Starting in January of that year, NWP members often marched in front of the White House, demanding the vote. They kept up their protests even after the United States entered World War I (1914–1918) in April. Wilson had some of the protesters arrested; the protesters then claimed that they were political prisoners—people arrested for their political beliefs, not for breaking the law.

Members of the National Woman's Party (NWP) marched in front of the White House often. Alice Paul, one of the NWP's founding members, can be seen holding the rear banner in this photograph of a march in 1917.

The NWP and its members were called militants, suggesting that they would use violence or radical means to achieve their goals. In some cases, they faced violence from police or other officials who did not like their methods. In November, after being arrested, several women were beaten by soldiers or police. In jail, the women refused to eat, and prison officials forced food into their stomachs. One woman later described how a doctor "forced the [feeding] tube through my lips and down my throat, I gasping and suffocating with the agony of it."

Famous Figures

ALICE PAUL
(1885-1977)

Like many of the early suffragists and abolitionists, Alice Paul belonged to the Society of Friends. The members of this Protestant church are called Quakers. Paul strongly accepted the Quaker belief that every person is equal in the eyes of God. In the early 1900s, while living in England, Paul saw that suffragists there were willing to use radical means to reach their goals. For example, women sometimes destroyed private property, risking arrest for their cause. Although Paul did not believe in using violence, she was ready to protest and go to jail, if necessary. From 1917 to 1921, Paul led the NWP. Once the Nineteenth Amendment was approved, she went to law school and then continued to work for equal rights for women in the United States and other countries.

Passing the Nineteenth Amendment

Although angry with Paul and the militants, Wilson was willing to work with Catt and the NAWSA. He saw that the suffrage movement would continue to grow. The war had also boosted the suffrage movement. The United States called on women to take traditionally male jobs as men joined the military. Women also risked their lives as war nurses. Their performance made it hard for Wilson and other politicians to deny them the right to vote.

In September 1918, Wilson voiced his support for a constitutional amendment ensuring women's suffrage. By this time, the U.S. House of Representatives had already approved such an amendment. In the Senate, however, it lost by two votes.

Congress addressed the issue again in the spring of 1919. This time, both houses passed the amendment, which then went to the states for their approval. Three-quarters of the forty-eight states in the country at that time had to ratify the amendment. Within a year, the suffragists won the support that they needed. In 1920 the Nineteenth Amendment was ratified, making women's suffrage part of the Constitution.

The Suffragists Argue Their Case

The suffragists of the early 1900s made some of the same arguments for suffrage that Stanton and the founders of the women's movement had made decades before. The United States was founded on the idea of equality—everyone had the same rights under the law. In practice, that idea was not always carried out, but it was a theory that Americans said they supported. One of the most important political rights that U.S. citizens enjoyed was the right to vote. To suggest that women could be citizens but not vote went against the values that had sparked the country's founding. Voting gives citizens some control over how their government is run and how society is shaped. Women, the suffragists said, were owed the right to play the same role in government and society that men did.

Fast Fact

Several countries, including Austria, Denmark, Finland, Germany, New Zealand, Poland, and Russia, adopted full female suffrage before the United States passed the Nineteenth Amendment.

The desire for some say in politics increased as more women took jobs outside the home. These workers lacked the political power to win support for laws that improved their lives. Melinda Scott, who worked in a New York factory, wrote, "I...want the ballot to be able to register my protest against the [working] conditions that are killing and maiming [workers]."

Some progressive suffragists appealed to the traditional view that women were good at taking care of others. When women had the vote, they could use their political power to reform social and political problems. One suffragist poster claimed that "women are by nature and training housekeepers. Let them help in the city housekeeping." This meant that with the vote, women could help get rid of corrupt local politicians and bring in better leaders.

The arguments for suffrage took on added weight once the United States entered World War I. President Wilson said that America was fighting to make the world safe for democracy. Carrie Chapman Catt and others argued that the United States should be just as concerned with extending democracy to all its own citizens. The best way to do that was to grant female suffrage. Catt wanted Wilson to support suffrage as a "war measure"— something that would help the country win the war. As one suffragist wrote to the president, giving women the vote would "enable [them] to throw yet more fully and whole-heartedly, their entire energy into work for their country...instead of for their own liberty and independence."

Alice Paul (second from left) and other members of the NWP hold a banner with a quote from Susan B. Anthony in June 1920 in Washington, D.C. They were about to attend the Republican National Convention, where they would rally in support of the Nineteenth Amendment, which was in the process of being ratified by the states.

In Their Own Words

Here is part of a 1915 leaflet from the National Woman Suffrage Publishing Company called "Twelve Reasons Why Women Should Vote."

1. *Because those who obey the laws should help to choose those who make the laws.*
2. *Because laws affect women as much as men.*
3. *Because laws which affect WOMEN are now passed without consulting them.*
4. *Because laws affecting CHILDREN should include the woman's point of view as well as the man's....*
10. *Because 8,000,000 women in the United States are wage workers, and the conditions under which they work are controlled by law.*
11. *Because the objections against their having the vote are based on prejudice, not on reason.*
12. *Because to sum up all reasons in one—IT IS FOR THE COMMON GOOD OF ALL.*

The Arguments against Suffrage

The people who opposed female suffrage included both men and women. Since they were anti-suffrage, or against suffrage, they were often called Antis. Like the suffrage supporters, they had a variety of reasons for opposing suffrage and the idea of women as equal to men.

With the birth of the women's movement in the nineteenth century, some Americans looked to the Bible to explain the ideal relationship between men and women. Many Christians believed that God had clearly meant for women to serve men. According to the Bible, they said, women gave up their rights, and in exchange, they received protection from men. Some ministers pointed specifically to Genesis, the first book of the Bible. God created man (Adam) first and then created woman (Eve) from a part of him—his rib. This showed, the ministers claimed, that man was more important to God than woman.

Throughout the nineteenth century and into the twentieth, many American men believed that women had only certain roles to play in society. The most important was being a wife and mother. Even as more women entered the workforce, a large number of Americans believed that women should focus on their families, not political affairs. In 1915, a Florida lawmaker who opposed suffrage said, "I prefer to look to the American woman as...the queen of the American home, instead of regarding her as a...politician in the cities."

Women, some Antis argued, already played a role in politics without actually having the right to vote. They could influence their husbands and other males in their family. Taking a more active role in politics would make women more like men, which, the critics said, was not a good thing. By nature, women and men were different. Women should accept that, instead of trying to be equal to men in every way.

Many of the female Antis did not believe that a "woman's place is in the home." They said that women could play many important roles in society, especially as social reformers. However, they said that women did not need the vote to accomplish good things. In a sense, they had more political clout without the vote. If men presented government leaders with a proposal, the politicians might refuse to act if the men did not belong to the same political party. The politicians might base their decisions on the potential for winning or losing votes in the future. Women, however, were nonpartisan—they did not belong to a party. Politicians would be more likely to consider their proposals and comments based on the worth of the ideas, not political concerns. An anti-suffrage newspaper wrote in 1908, "Outside the political machinery, there is a world...where all reform begins."

Fast Fact

Formal anti-suffrage groups first formed during the 1860s. During the first decade of the twentieth century, the most important of these groups was the National Association Opposed to Woman Suffrage, which was founded by women.

Some people joined the anti-suffrage movement because they disliked the suffragists and their values. Some immigrants and Roman Catholics disliked the nativism of suffragist leaders such as Catt. The liquor industry opposed suffrage because so many of the suffragists wanted prohibition, or the banning of alcohol. Suffragists were also sometimes associated with people who supported socialism. Under this economic system, the government owns most or all businesses. Americans who opposed socialism tended to oppose women's suffrage.

Some of the Antis' beliefs endured in the United States even after the passage of the Nineteenth Amendment. With the right to vote, women had their first chance to run for political office, but the number of women elected to top government positions was and remains low. As of 2004, just 74 out of the 535 members of the U.S. Congress were women, and neither of the two major political parties had ever chosen a woman to run for president. In the 1984 election, the Democrats chose Geraldine Ferraro to run as their vice presidential candidate, but she and running mate Walter Mondale lost the election.

In Their Own Words

Here is part of a statement from the Nebraska Association Opposed to Woman Suffrage, published in 1914.

The great majority of intelligent, refined and educated women do not want [suffrage].... They have all the rights and freedoms they desire, and consider their present trusts most sacred and important. They feel that the duties which naturally must ever [fall on] their sex are such that none but themselves can perform and that political responsibilities could not be borne by them without the sacrifice of the highest interests of their families and of society.

CHAPTER TWELVE

The New Deal

WHAT
President Franklin D. Roosevelt introduces a package
of programs to limit the effects of the Great Depression.

ISSUE
The amount of influence that the federal government
should have on the economy

WHERE
Nationwide

WHEN
1933–1935

*D*uring most of the 1920s, the United States enjoyed a strong economy. People called the decade "the Roaring Twenties." Mass production, first perfected by automaker Henry Ford, let companies produce more goods at a lower cost. Productivity rose, meaning that a company could use fewer workers than before to make more goods. Workers also earned higher salaries than they did in the years before World War I (1914–1918). Radios and household appliances such as refrigerators joined cars as new items that most Americans wanted to buy. The advertising industry convinced consumers that they needed these items, which they could buy on credit.

Americans also used their income to invest in stocks. Companies sell stock, or shares, in their company to raise money. The shareholders then own small pieces of the company and earn money if the company does well. If a company loses money, however, stock prices fall and the shareholders' investments lose value. During the 1920s, many stock prices rose, and investors believed that they would keep rising. Some investors also borrowed money to buy stocks, thinking that they could one day pay off the loans when their stocks became more valuable.

Three Republicans—Warren G. Harding, Calvin Coolidge, and Herbert Hoover—served as president during these boom years. In general, they believed that the federal government should not be too involved in the economy. Capitalism, the U.S. economic system, worked best when it was as free as possible. The Republican leaders also favored lowering taxes for businesses and the wealthy, so that they would have more money to invest in new industries. In 1928, while running for president, Hoover told voters that the Republican policies of the 1920s had "come nearer to the abolition of poverty...than humanity has ever reached before." The country, he argued, could eliminate poverty altogether if it stayed on the same path.

EASY MONEY

The boom of the 1920s was fueled partially by what is called "cheap money" or "easy money." In 1913, Congress had created the Federal Reserve System, a series of regional banks for the country run by the Federal Reserve Board. This board makes financial decisions on its own, but Congress can review its actions. The Federal Reserve System sets the interest rates that banks can charge each other, and that rate influences the rates that banks charge their customers. During the 1920s, the Federal Reserve System kept interest rates low, making it easier for businesses and consumers to borrow money. The low rates helped U.S. companies invest in Europe, which had been devastated by World War I. However, the cheap money also encouraged heavy borrowing at home, which led to problems after 1929.

Trouble under the Surface

Despite Hoover's view and the money that so many Americans were making, the U.S. economy was not as strong as it looked. For most of the decade, farmers increased their productivity. As they produced more crops, the price for those goods fell, meaning that the farmers made less money. Rising productivity also affected workers in some industries. Companies made more money as they produced more goods, but they did not always raise their employees' salaries. By the end of the 1920s, stores had more goods than consumers could afford to buy, even with credit. Companies then began firing workers to save money, so a growing number of families had even less money to spend.

As business weakened, the price of stocks began to fall. When this happened, some investors tried to sell their stocks to repay loans that they had taken to buy the stocks in the first place. More people then began to sell, pushing the stock value even lower. The stock market gains of the 1920s had been based on speculation, or the idea that prices will always rise—yet the economy always runs in cycles, with bad times following the booms. Vincent Sheean, a journalist of the era, wrote that "thousands of people must have known that a speculative boom...would be followed by a terrible crash, and yet...nobody spoke up loudly."

That stock market crash came in the fall of 1929. On October 24, stock prices began to tumble. Five days later, on a day nicknamed "Black Thursday," the stock market lost about $14 billion in value. Many people who had invested heavily in stocks lost most or all of their savings.

When people lost their jobs or investments in the stock market, they tried to withdraw money that they had saved at local banks. Often, many people tried to withdraw their money at the same time, and the banks did not have enough money on hand to give them. The banks had invested their customers' savings in companies or projects that had lost money. These so-called bank runs forced many banks to go out of business, and investors lost their savings. This problem continued through Hoover's presidency, reaching its peak at the end of 1932.

Hoover's Response

The stock market crash marked the beginning of a long economic downturn called the Great Depression. At first, President Hoover tried to reassure Americans that the economic problems were not as bad as they seemed. On October 25, just before Black Thursday, he said, "The fundamental business of the country...is on a sound and prosperous basis."

Unlike Coolidge before him, Hoover was willing for the U.S. government to play some role in the economy. Among other measures, the president asked Congress to create a new government agency, the Reconstruction Finance Corporation (RFC). This agency loaned money to banks and insurance companies to help them stay in business. However, Hoover refused to give direct federal government aid to individuals. He thought that private charities, along with state and local programs, would be enough to help the growing number of unemployed people.

AN INTERNATIONAL PROBLEM

In 1930, President Hoover supported the Smoot-Hawley Tariff. A tariff is a tax on imported goods. The tariff raised the price of certain foreign goods so that consumers would be more likely to buy products made in the United States. Governments in Europe responded by placing their own tariffs on U.S. goods, which hurt American companies selling overseas. In addition, the tariff hurt the economy in European nations, so European workers had less money to buy U.S. goods.

The results of World War I also played a role in making the Great Depression a worldwide problem. The United States and its allies, including France and Great Britain, had defeated a group of nations led by Germany. After the war, the French and British required the Germans to pay reparations to the Allies—money to make up for the property that the Germans had destroyed during the war. These reparations were too high for the Germans to afford, and their economy crumbled. The French and British, meanwhile, were counting on getting the money from Germany so they could repay loans that they had borrowed from the United States. Without the reparations, they could not repay their loans or invest money in their own countries. The lack of money also hurt their colonies and their trade with other nations. The effects of the Great Depression were thus felt around the world.

The New Deal

In 1932, Hoover ran for reelection. His opponent was Franklin D. Roosevelt, the Democratic governor of New York. Roosevelt wanted the federal government to play a larger role in the economy, especially in giving aid to the poor and unemployed.

American voters were tired of Hoover's policy, and Roosevelt easily won the presidential election.

Roosevelt quickly took action to address the effects of the Great Depression. The series of programs that he supported were known as the New Deal. The new agencies that he created included the Agricultural Adjustment Administration, which helped farmers, and the Civilian Conservation Corps, which hired young men to work in parks and forests. To address concerns about how the stock market was run, Congress created the Security and Exchange Commission (SEC), while the Federal Deposit Insurance Corporation (FDIC) protected the money that investors placed in banks. Roosevelt also tried to convince businesses to set limits on the prices that they charged for their goods, and for the first time, the U.S. government gave direct aid to the unemployed.

Roosevelt's first round of programs are now called the First New Deal. In 1935, he launched a Second New Deal to address the continuing problems of the Great Depression. The new programs included the Works Progress Administration, which eventually hired 8 million Americans to build roads and airports, create art for public buildings, and perform other jobs that benefited the country. Another key program was Social Security, an insurance system run by the government. Working people and businesses paid into the Social Security fund so that those who were unemployed, elderly, retired, or disabled could receive money when they needed it.

Roosevelt was reelected in 1936, and the New Deal era lasted through the decade. Roosevelt's programs did not end the Great Depression, but they softened the crisis that many people faced. World War II (1939–1945) played a larger role in putting Americans back to work, as the government spent billions of dollars on weapons and supplies.

THE NUMBERS ON UNEMPLOYMENT

When Roosevelt was sworn in as president in March 1933, an estimated 12 million Americans were unemployed—about one-third of the people who were willing and able to work. By 1941, the unemployment rate was still close to 10 percent. In contrast, after the recession of 2001 and 2002, about 6 percent of Americans were unemployed. Economists say that no country can ever have full employment. An unemployment rate of about 4 percent is considered the sign of a healthy economy.

Works Progress Administration (WPA) workers build a sidewalk in New Jersey in 1938. The WPA was one of the New Deal programs started by President Franklin Roosevelt during the Great Depression in order to create jobs and ease the effects of the weak economy.

Roosevelt Argues for the New Deal

Since the nineteenth century, U.S. leaders had promoted laissez-faire economics, a system that rested on the idea that the government should not pass laws that restricted what businesses did. Many Americans also opposed the federal government owning businesses or creating social programs that tried to redistribute wealth, or take money from the wealthy to help the poor. Those kinds of government actions seemed too close to socialism, an economic system in which the government owns businesses and controls the economy. Most Americans believed that socialism was a threat to their values of political democracy and personal freedom.

> *Fast Fact*
>
> *Laissez-faire* is French for "allow to do."

To Roosevelt, one of Hoover's basic faults was refusing to take enough government action during the Great Depression. Roosevelt worked with a group of advisers called the Brain Trust, most of whom had worked at well-known universities. They argued that the U.S. economy had drastically changed since the mid-nineteenth century, because of mass production and the rise of huge, powerful corporations.

Roosevelt and the Brain Trust realized that the economy always went through good times and bad. Now, however, the bad times were extremely severe and required government action to soften the effects on the average person. Adolf Berle Jr., one of Roosevelt's advisers, wrote in 1933 that if the country waited for the situation to improve on its own, "You may have half of the entire country begging in the streets or starving to death."

Roosevelt believed that his New Deal was a middle ground between the extreme government control of the economy under socialism and the laissez-faire policies of the past. He knew that the New Deal was unlike any program that the U.S. government had tried before, but the Great Depression was unlike past economic problems. Roosevelt also believed that his efforts were true to the spirit of American government as spelled out in the

U.S. Constitution. He told Americans that a "combination of the old and the new...marks orderly progress."

Roosevelt admitted that his New Deal programs were experiments—some would work and some would not—but he believed that most Americans were willing to try something new. The people who criticized the New Deal, Roosevelt said, were Americans who expected some kind of special privilege but no longer received it. He called these people "a selfish minority" who "think of themselves first and their fellow beings second."

In Their Own Words

Roosevelt's supporters included Boston department store owner Edward Filene. In 1934, Filene wrote an article that defended the New Deal. Here is part of what he wrote.

The New Deal, as I see it, is a movement toward a nation-wide economic constitution.... If we want to go on with democracy, and I am sure we do, the New Deal points the way.... It isn't a question of whether business shall or shall not be operated under a code [of requirements].... It is merely a question of whether our big-community business can operate under the old, little-community code, and it has been amply proved that it cannot.

Opposing the New Deal

Even before he lost the 1932 election to Roosevelt, Herbert Hoover attacked the Democratic Party's proposed response to the Great Depression. The New Deal, Hoover argued, would mean more government control and a loss of freedom. Most critics of the New Deal had similar concerns. To them, the old policy of laissez-faire had made the U.S. economy strong.

The most vocal critics of the New Deal were business owners and wealthy people. In 1934, a group of business leaders formed the American Liberty League to try to stop New Deal programs. The league wanted to prevent any government efforts to deny rights guaranteed under the Constitution, especially rights relating to owning and using private property. League members claimed that the New Deal limited personal freedom and interfered with property rights and that those limitations would lead to socialism in the United States. The league's president, Jarrett Shouse, wrote in 1934 that "governmental disregard for property rights soon leads to disregard for other rights."

Some opponents also feared giving direct government aid to the poor, because the poor might not work as hard or save for the future if they thought that the government would help them out in any crisis. Newton D. Baker was one person who held this view. He had served in the cabinet of President Woodrow Wilson and later worked for companies on Wall Street. Baker said that New Deal programs were a "sad discouragement to those who worked hard, kept out of debt and saved modest [amounts] for their old age."

Baker and other Americans also feared the growth of the federal government that would be needed to carry out new federal policies and programs. These people believed that the best government was close to the people that it governed. Voters had more contact with local and state officials than with federal officials and so could watch the actions of those officials and correct mistakes. Critics feared that a huge federal bureaucracy would not respond to citizens' needs and would have too much control over their lives.

Not all Roosevelt's critics were conservative. Socialists and others who disliked the role that big business played in American society also attacked the New Deal. To them, the programs did not go far enough in limiting corporate power and helping the poor and working classes. One person who wanted the government to do more was Senator Huey Long of Louisiana. He proposed a program called Share Our Wealth, which would sharply increase taxes on the wealthy and give the money to the poor. "America," he said, "cannot allow the multi-millionaires and the billionaires, a mere handful of them, to own everything."

The attacks on the New Deal from both conservatives and radicals led Roosevelt to change some of his programs. He wanted to win support from people who backed more extreme groups and leaders. To do this, he borrowed some of their ideas. Also at times, the U.S. Supreme Court struck down New Deal laws, declaring that they were unconstitutional. Many programs, however, such as Social Security and government control of the stock market, remain in place today. The debate over the role of the government in the economy that started with the New Deal also continues.

Famous Figures

HUEY LONG
(1893–1935)

Huey Long was one of the most loved—and hated—U.S. politicians of the 1930s. Long was elected governor of Louisiana in 1928. He carried out a successful reform program that built roads, schools, and hospitals in Louisiana's rural regions while raising taxes on the rich. Long used his popularity to influence all areas of his state's government, going beyond the legal power that he held as governor. His corrupt ways led Long's critics to call him a dictator.

Long was elected to the U.S. Senate in 1930 and two years later supported Roosevelt for president. However, Long thought that the New Deal did not do enough to help the poor. Long was killed in 1935 by a political foe from Louisiana.

Herbert Hoover is pictured at the Republican National Convention in Cleveland, Ohio, in 1936, where he sharply criticized President Roosevelt's New Deal programs.

In Their Own Words

In 1936, Herbert Hoover was still the best-known Republican in the United States, even though he no longer held political office. During the presidential campaign that year, he often spoke out against Roosevelt and the New Deal while promoting the Republican party. Here is part of one of his speeches.

The New Dealers say that all this that we propose is a worn-out system; that this machine age requires new measures for which we must sacrifice some part of the freedom of men. Men have lost their way with the confused ideas that governments should run machines. Man-made machines cannot be of more worth than men themselves. Free men made these machines. Only free spirits can master them to their proper use.... Let me say to you that any measure which breaks our [walls] of freedom will flood the land with misery.

Glossary

allies—friends and supporters of a person or country

ambassador—a person who represents a government in a foreign country

amendment—a change or addition to a legal document

avenge—to make up for a wrongful action by punishing the person who did it

bureaucracy—workers and officials who run the daily affairs of a government agency; they are not elected

cabinet—a group of advisers to a leader

civil rights—legal rights relating to political and legal activities, such as the right to vote

conservative—someone who approves of the traditional ways of doing things and does not want to change

corporate—relating to large businesses

corruption—the use of illegal methods to gain money or power

delegate—a person chosen to represent others at a meeting or convention

discrimination—the unequal treatment of a person or group based on such traits as race, ethnic background, sex, or religion

dissenting—opposing the beliefs held by a majority

distilleries—companies that make strong alcoholic drinks such as whiskey, rum, and vodka

domestic—relating to issues or products within a country's borders

fraud—crime involving deception in order to steal money

imperialism—the policy of extending a nation's authority by acquiring overseas territories or establishing economic control over overseas territories

inauguration—the ceremony giving an elected presidential candidate the powers of the office

mechanized—done by machinery

militia—a part-time military force composed of local volunteers

moral—correct, as defined by religious or legal teachings

morale—the mental or emotional attitude of a group

radical—extreme in thoughts or actions, compared to most members of a community

ratify—to formally approve a suggested action

ration—to limit how much people can buy or use of a certain product

repeal—to overturn a law

resolution—a statement of belief or desire to take action

secede—to formally withdraw from a political organization

testimony—statements made during a court case

transcontinental—stretching across a continent

Bibliography

BOOKS

Burgan, Michael. *Henry Ford: Industrialist*. Chicago: Ferguson Publishing, 2001.

Collier, Christopher, and James Collier. *The Rise of Industry, 1860–1900*. New York: Benchmark Books, 2000.

Dolan, Edward F. *The Spanish-American War*. Brookfield, CT: Millbrook Press, 2001.

Dumbeck, Kristina. *Leaders of Women's Suffrage*. San Diego: Lucent Books, 2001.

Hanes, Sharon M., and Richard C. Hanes. *Great Depression and New Deal Almanac*. Detroit: UXL, 2002.

Lucas, Eileen. *The Eighteenth and Twenty-First Amendments: Alcohol, Prohibition, and Repeal*. Springfield, NJ: Enslow Publishers, 1998.

Perl, Lila. *To the Golden Mountain: The Story of the Chinese Who Built the Transcontinental Railroad*. New York: Benchmark Books, 2003.

Rogers, James T. *Woodrow Wilson: Visionary for Peace*. New York: Facts on File, 1997.

Wormser, Richard. *The Rise and Fall of Jim Crow*. New York: Franklin Watts, 1999.

WEB SITES

Anti-Saloon League 1893–1933 *www.wpl.lib.oh.us/AntiSaloon/*

Crucible of Empire—The Spanish-American War *www.pbs.org/crucible/*

The Dramas of Haymarket *www.chicagohistory.org/dramas/index.htm*

The Great War and the Shaping of the 20th Century *www.pbs.org/greatwar/*

HarpWeek—Finding Precedent: Hayes vs. Tilden, The Electoral College Controversy of 1876–1877 *www.elections.harpweek.com/controversy.htm*

The Internet Public Library—Presidents of the United States *www.ipl.org/div/potus/*Women and Social Movements in the United States, 1775–2000 *www.binghamton.edu/womhist/datelist.htm*

Cumulative Index

A

AAPA. *See* Association Against the Prohibition Amendment
AASS. *See* American Anti-Slavery Society
abolitionists
    Vol. 2: 114–122
    Vol. 3: 62–63, 89, 102, 103
    Vol. 4: 110
abortion
    Vol. 1: 9
    Vol. 2: 9
    Vol. 3: 9
    Vol. 4: 9
    Vol. 5: 8, 9, 62, 62–74, 66, 68, 70, 73, 85
absentee ballot, Vol. 5: 125
Adams, Abigail
    Vol. 1: 100, *100*
    Vol. 3: 52
Adams, John
    Vol. 1: 75, 87, 94, 95, 96, 98
    Vol. 2: *33*, 33–34
Adams, John Quincy
    Vol. 2: 106, 108–112
    Vol. 3: 109
Adams, Samuel, Vol. 1: 83, 87–88, 89
Addams, Jane, Vol. 4: 88
affirmative action, Vol. 5: 100–110, *101, 103, 104, 107*
African Americans
    Vol. 3:
        Andrew Johnson and, 123, 124
        civil rights for, *112*, 112–120, *116*
        freeing of the slaves, 102–110, *105, 108*
        secession of Southern states and, *92*, 92–100, *94, 97*
    Vol. 4:
        election of 1876 and, 13, 14, 17, 19
        Plessy v. Ferguson, 52, 52–58, *54*
        Republican policy toward, 12
        in suffragist movement, 112
    Vol. 5:
        affirmative action and, 100, 102, 107–108, 109, 110
        Brown v. Board of Education, 36–46, *38, 44*
        election of 2000 and, 129
        Vietnam War and, 59
Agricultural Adjustment Administration, Vol. 4: 126
Aguinaldo, Emilio, Vol. 4: 68
alcohol, Vol. 4: 100–108, *101, 106*

Alexander, James, Vol. 1: 53
Alien and Sedition Acts, Vol. 2: 24–30Alien Enemies Act, Vol. 2: 24–25, 28–29
alimony, Vol. 5: 84
Allen, John, Vol. 2: 29
Allies
    Vol. 1: 133
    Vol. 5: 133. *See also* Triple Entente
Almond, Lincoln, Vol. 5: *123*
Altgeld, John Peter, Vol. 4: 47, 49
AMA. *See* American Medical Association
Amalgamated Society of Engineers, Vol. 4: 46
ambassador, Vol. 5: 133
Amelia (factory worker), Vol. 2: 103
amendment
    Vol. 1: 128, 133
    Vol. 5: 133. *See also* specific amendments
American Anti-Slavery Society (AASS), Vol. 2: 117 Vol. 3: 53
An American Dilemma (Myrdal), Vol. 5: 43
American Liberty League, Vol. 4: 130
American Medical Association (AMA), Vol. 5: 64
American Revolution, Vol. 1: 80–90, 84, 86
American Slavery As It Is (Weld), Vol. 2: 121
American System
    Vol. 2: 124
    Vol. 4: 73
American Woman Suffrage Association (AWSA), Vol. 4: 110, 112
amicus curiae briefs, Vol. 5: 106, 107
ammunition, Vol. 1: 133
anarchists, Vol. 4: 43, 44–50
Anglicanism, Vol. 1: 60
annexation of Texas, Vol. 3: 32–40
Anthony, Susan B.
    Vol. 3: 119
    Vol. 4: 110, 111
anti-communism, Vol. 5: 24–34, *27, 28, 30*
anti-Federalists, Vol. 1: 125–132
Anti-Saloon League (ASL), Vol. 4: 101, 102–103, 105
anti-suffrage movement, Vol. 4: 118–120
Antis, Vol. 4: 118–120
antiwar movement, Vol. 5: *51*, 51, 57–60, 59
An Appeal to the Colored People of the World (Walker), Vol. 2: 116

armory
    Vol. 3: 133
    Vol. 4: 133
Articles of Confederation, Vol. 1: 104–112, *108*, 114–122
ASL. *See* Anti-Saloon League
assembly centers, Vol. 5: 14–15
assembly lines, Vol. 4: 72
Association Against the Prohibition Amendment (AAPA), Vol. 4: 107, 108
Association for the Study of Abortion, Vol. 5: 65
atomic bomb, Vol. 5: 26, 29
atonement, Vol. 1: 133
Austin, Stephen, Vol. 3: 32
Austria-Hungary, Vol. 4: 80
automobile industry, Vol. 4: 70, 70–78, *71, 76*
AWSA. *See* American Woman Suffrage Association

B

B & O. *See* Baltimore and Ohio Railroad
Bacon, Nathaniel, Vol. 1: 33–40, *35, 36*
Bacon's Rebellion, Vol. 1: 32–40, *35, 36*
Baker, Newton D., Vol. 4: 130
Bakke, Allan, Vol. 5: *101,* 101–103, 103
Ball, George, Vol. 5: 59
ballot, Vol. 5: 124–132, *128, 133*
Baltimore and Ohio Railroad (B & O), Vol. 4: 24–25, 28
Bank of the United States (BUS), Vol. 3: 22–30, *23*
Bank War. *See* Bank of the United States
Baptist church, Vol. 1: 15, 64–65, 67
Battle of Buena Vista, Vol. 3: 45
Beecher, Henry Ward, Vol. 4: 29
Bell, John, Vol. 3: 94, *94*
Bennett, William, Vol. 5: 119
Bentley, Elizabeth, Vol. 5: 28
Benton, Thomas Hart, Vol. 3: 24
Berkeley, William, Vol. 1: 32–40
Berle, Adolf, Jr., Vol. 4: 128
Beveridge, Albert, Vol. 4: 66
Bible, Vol. 4: 118–119
Biddle, Francis, Vol. 5: 20–21
Biddle, Nicholas, Vol. 3: 24, 25
Bill of Rights, Vol. 1: 125, 128
Bingham, John A., Vol. 3: 117
Bishop, Bridget, Vol. 1: 45
Black Codes
    Vol. 3: 113, 114, 117
    Vol. 4: 52–53
    Vol. 5: 42
Black Hawk, Vol. 3: *16*
Black, Hugo, Vol. 5: 19
Blackmun, Harry, Vol. 5: 67, 71
Blackstone, William, Vol. 3: 60

"Black Thursday," Vol. 4: 124
Blatch, Harriet Stanton,
    Vol. 4: 113
blockades, Vol. 2: 64–65
Bok, Derek, Vol. 5: 106–107
Boland Amendment, Vol. 5:
    90–91
Boland, Edward, Vol. 5: 91
Boland II, Vol. 5: 91, 95
Bollinger, Lee, Vol. 5: 104
Bolton, John, Vol. 5: *128*
Bonaparte, Napoleon,
    Vol. 2: 44, 45
bootlegging, Vol. 4: 104, 108
Borah, William, Vol. 4: 95
Border Ruffians, Vol. 3: 75
Boston (MA), Vol. 1: 80–83
Boston Manufacturing Company,
    Vol. 2: 97–98
Boston Massacre, Vol. 1: 80
Boston Tea Party, Vol. 1: 80, 81
Boutwell, George, Vol. 3: 128
Bradford, William, Vol. 1: 17,
    53, 55
Bradley, Joseph, Vol. 4: *18*, 18, 53
Bradley, Richard,
    Vol. 1: 54, 55, 56
Brain Trust, Vol. 4: 128
Brattle, Thomas, Vol. 1: 49–50
Breckenridge, John, Vol. 3: 93,
    94, 94
Brennan, William
    Vol. 1: 9
    Vol. 2: 9
    Vol. 3: 9
    Vol. 4: 9
    Vol. 5: 9
Briggs, Harry, Vol. 5: 38, 44
Briggs v. Elliot, Vol. 5: 38–39, 42
Brown, Henry Billings, Vol. 4: 58
Brown, John, Vol. 3: 76
Brown, Linda, Vol. 5: 39, *44*
Brown v. Board of Education,
    Vol. 5: 38, 39–46, *44*, 67, 100
Buchanan, James, Vol. 3: 88, 99
Bumpers, Dale, Vol. 5: 120
Burke, Edmund, Vol. 1: 90
Burke, Thomas, Vol. 1: 112
Burlingame, Anson, Vol. 4: 34
Burlingame Treaty, Vol. 4: 34
Burr, Aaron, Vol. 2: 37, 52–62, *61*
Burr Conspiracy, Vol. 2: 52–62
Burton, Charles, Vol. 5: *128*
BUS. *See* Bank of the
    United States
Bush, George H.W.
    Vol. 5:
        affirmative action
            and, 105
        defeat by
            Bill Clinton, 112
        George W. Bush and, 122
        internment of Japanese
            Americans and, 18
        Iran-Contra affair and,
            94, 95
Bush, George W.
    Vol. 4: 20
    Vol. 5: 122–132
Bush, Jeb, Vol. 5: 122
Bush v. Gore, Vol. 5: 130

butterfly ballot,
    Vol. 5: 128, 129, 131

C
cabinet
    Vol. 3: 133
    Vol. 4: 133
    Vol. 5: 133
Calef, Robert, Vol. 1: 50
Calhoun, John C.
    Vol. 2: 82, 124–125,
        125, 129
    Vol. 3: 37–38, 48, 67–69
California
    Vol. 3: 63, 64
    Vol. 4: 32–40, *33, 37, 38*
    Vol. 5: 12, 109
Calvinists, Vol. 1: 12–20
Calvin, John, Vol. 1: 12
Cambodia, Vol. 5: 53
Camp Upton, Long Island (NY),
    Vol. 4: 84
capitalism, Vol. 4: 28–29, 122
Caprio, Joyce E., Vol. 5: *123*
Carroll, Charles, Vol. 1: 111
Catt, Carrie Chapman, Vol. 4:
    113, 117
CEA. *See* Constitutional
    Equality Amendment
censure, Vol. 3: 29
Center for Individual Rights
    (CIR), Vol. 5: 103–104, 109
Central Intelligence Agency
    (CIA), Vol. 5: 89, 91, 94
Central Pacific Railroad,
    Vol. 4: 32, *33*
Central Powers. *See* Triple
    Alliance (the Central Powers)
chad, Vol. 5: 128
Chambers, Whittaker,
    Vol. 5: 26, *27*
Charles I, King of England,
    Vol. 1: 13
Charles II, King of England,
    Vol. 1: 37, 38, 39
charter, Vol. 1: 133
Chase, Salmon, Vol. 3: 79–80
Chase, Samuel, Vol. 1: 106, 109
Chauncy, Charles, Vol. 1: 67, 68
Cherokee, Vol. 3: 12–13, 14–15
Chickasaw, Vol. 3: 14
China, Vol. 5: 48, 54, 55–56, 91
Chinese Exclusion Act,
    Vol. 4: 32–40, *33, 37, 38*
Chisholm, Shirley, Vol. 5: 83
Choctaw, Vol. 3: 14
Christianity, Vol. 1: 60–68, *62, 64*
Christians, Vol. 1: 42–50
CIA. *See* Central
    Intelligence Agency
CIR. *See* Center for
    Individual Rights
civil rights
    Vol. 3: *112,* 112–120, *116*
    Vol. 5: 133
Civil Rights Act of 1866
    Vol. 3: 113–114, 119, 124
Civil Rights Act of 1875
    Vol. 4: 53–54
Civil Rights Act of 1964,
    Vol. 5: 100, 101, 104

Civil War, Vol. 3: 96–100,
    103–104, 105
Civilian Conservation Corps,
    Vol. 4: 126
Clark, Kenneth, Vol. 5: 42
Clay, Henry
    Vol. 2:
        American System and,
            124
        elections of 1824 and,
            107–112
        Missouri Compromise
            and, 89, 90
        nullification and,
            128–129
        political history of, 81
        portrait of, *110*
    Vol. 3:
        BUS and, 24–25
        Compromise of 1850 and,
            66–67, 68, 69–70
Cleveland, Grover, Vol. 4: 60
Clinton, Bill
    Vol. 3: 126
    Vol. 5:
        Al Gore and, 122
        Fred Korematsu and, *21*
        impeachment of,
            112–120, *115, 117*
        Travelgate, 89
Clinton, Hillary Rodham,
    Vol. 5: 112
Coercive Acts, Vol. 1: 80
Coffee, Linda, Vol. 5: 66
Cold War
    Vol. 5:
        anti-Communism, 24–34,
            27, 28, 30
        Iran-Contra affair and,
            88–89
        Vietnam War and, 48, 54,
            55–56
Coleman, Mary Sue, Vol. 5: 105
colleges, Vol. 1: 63. *See also*
    universities, affirmative
    action in
Common Sense (Paine), Vol. 1:
    97–98, 99, 101
communication
    Vol. 1: 9
    Vol. 2: 9
    Vol. 3: 9
    Vol. 4: 9
    Vol. 5: 9
communism
    Vol. 4: 28–29
    Vol. 5:
        Cold War anti-
            Communism, 24–34,
            27, 28, 30
        Iran-Contra affair and,
            88–89
        Vietnam War and, 48,
            49–50, 52, 54, 55–56
The Communist Manifesto (Marx
    and Engels), Vol. 4: 43
Compromise of 1850, Vol. 3:
    62–70, 68
Concord (MA), Vol. 1: 83, 84–85
Confederacy, Vol. 3: 96–100

Confederate States of America, Vol. 3: 96–100, 102
confederation, Vol. 1: 133
Congregationalism, Vol. 1: 18, 60, 61–68
Congregationalists. *See* Puritans
Congress. *See* U.S. Congress
conservative, Vol. 5: 133
conspiracy
    Vol. 3: 133
    Vol. 4: 133
Constitution, U.S.
    Vol. 1: 124–131, *127, 132*
    Vol. 2: 86
    Vol. 3: 92, 102
    Vol. 5: 131
Constitutional Convention, Vol. 1: 107–108, 113–122, *118, 121*
Constitutional Equality Amendment (CEA), Vol. 5: 81
Constitutional Union Party, Vol. 3: 94
Continental Army, Vol. 1: 92
Continental Congress, Vol. 1: 94–98, 102, 104–106
contras, Vol. 5: 89, 91, 94
Coolidge, Calvin, Vol. 4: 122
Cooper, Thomas, Vol. 2: 103
Corey, Giles, Vol. 1: 45
"corrupt bargain," Vol. 2: 109–112
corruption
    Vol. 1: 133
    Vol. 3: 133
    Vol. 4: 133
    Vol. 5: 133
Cosby, William, Vol. 1: 52–54, 55
Cotton, John, Vol. 1: 17–18, 19, *19*
Craig, Gregory, Vol. 5: *115*
Crawford, William, Vol. 2: 106
Creek, Vol. 3: 14
Crittenden, John, Vol. 3: 95, 100
Cuba, Vol. 4: 60–68, *61, 63*
Cunningham, Milton J., Vol. 4: 57–58
Currie, Bettie, Vol. 5: 114
Czechoslovakia, Vol. 5: 26

D
Daughters of Liberty, Vol. 1: 73
Davenport, James, Vol. 1: 66, 68
Davis, Jefferson, Vol. 3: 96
Davis, John W., Vol. 5: 44–45
Dawes, William, Vol. 1: 83
Deane, Silas, Vol. 1: 104
The Death of Outrage (Bennett), Vol. 5: 119
death penalty, Vol. 1: 42
debatable issues
    Vol. 1: 7–9
    Vol. 2: 7–9
    Vol. 3: 7–9
    Vol. 4: 7–9
    Vol. 5: 7–9
Declaration of Independence
    Vol. 1:
        Abigail Adams, *100*
        arguments against independence, 99–102
        debate for independence, 95–99

precursors to, 92–94
    writing of, 94–95, 96
"Declaration of the Causes and Necessity of Taking Up Arms" (Dickinson and Jefferson), Vol. 1: 92
"Declaration in the Name of the People" (Bacon), Vol. 1: 38
"Declaration of Rights and Sentiments" (Stanton)
    Vol. 3: 58
    Vol. 4: 110
Declaratory Act, Vol. 1: 77–78
DeJarnette, Daniel, Vol. 3: 98
Delancey, James, Vol. 1: 53, 54, 55–56
Delancey, Stephen, Vol. 1: 52
de Lôme, Enrique Dupuy, Vol. 4: 62
Democratic Party
    Vol. 3:
        civil rights for African Americans and, 117, 119
        Compromise of 1850 and, 67, 69
        emancipation and, 106
        slavery and, 93
        Texas annexation and, 36–38
        Thirteenth Amendment and, 109
    Vol. 4:
        Chinese and, 36
        election of 1876 and, 12–20
        League of Nations and, 93–94
        Prohibition and, 104
    Vol. 5: 116, 117, 122–132
Democratic-Republican Party
    Vol. 2:
        Alien and Sedition Acts and, 25–28
        defense of Embargo Acts, 69–70
        elections issues of 1800, 38–40
        Jay's Treaty and, 15–16, 17, 20
        overview of, 12
        War of 1812 and, 81–82, 84
        XYZ affair and, 23
depression, Vol. 3: 22
despotism
    Vol. 1: 133
    Vol. 3: 133
    Vol. 4: 133
Detroit Free Press, Vol. 3: 78
Dewey, George, Vol. 4: 63
DeWitt, John, Vol. 5: 19, 21
Dickens, Charles, Vol. 2: 104
Dickinson, John, Vol. 1: 92, 93, 102, 105
Diem, Ngo Dinh, Vol. 5: 49, 50, 51
discrimination
    Vol. 3: 133
    Vol. 4: 133
    Vol. 5: 133.

See also racism; reverse discrimination
dissenting
    Vol. 3: 133
    Vol. 4: 133
    Vol. 5: 133
disunion, Vol. 3: 64
Doe v. Bolton, Vol. 5: 67
Donelson, Andrew Jackson, Vol. 2: 111
Douglass, Frederick, Vol. 3: 54, 103
Douglas, Stephen
    Vol. 3:
        in election of 1860, 93, *94,* 94
        Kansas-Nebraska Act of, 73
        Nebraska Territory and, 77
        portrait of, *79*
        secession of Southern states and, 100
Douglas, William O., Vol. 5: 34
draft, Vol. 5: 58, 59
Dred Scott case, Vol. 3: 82–90, *83*
Duane, William, Vol. 3: 25
Du Bois, W.E.B., Vol. 5: 45
due process, Vol. 4: 56, 57–58
Durbin, Richard, Vol. 5: 120
Dutch Reformed Church, Vol. 1: 60, 64

E
Easton, John, Vol. 1: 29
economy (1930s), Vol. 4: 122–132
education
    Vol. 5:
        affirmative action, 100–110, *101, 103, 104, 107*
        Brown v. Board of Education, 36–46, *38, 44*
Edwards, Jonathan, Vol. 1: 62, *62,* 63, 65
Eighteenth Amendment, Vol. 4: 102–103, *106, 107*
Eisenhower, Dwight, Vol. 5: 46, 49, 56
election of 1800, Vol. 2: 32–40
election of 1824, Vol. 2: 106–112, *107*
election of 1876, Vol. 4: 12–20, *13, 16, 18*
election of 2000. *See* presidential election of 2000
Electoral College
    Vol. 2: 35
    Vol. 5: *123*
Electoral Commission, Vol. 4: *16,* 16–20
electoral vote
    Vol. 4: 14–20
    Vol. 5: 123
electors, Vol. 2: 34, 35
Elliot, Roderick, Vol. 5: 38
Ellsberg, Daniel, Vol. 5: 60
El Salvador, Vol. 5: 88–89, 90

"Emancipation Proclamation" (Lincoln), Vol. 3: 104–107
embargo, Vol. 5: 133
Embargo of 1808, Vol. 2: 8, 64–72
Emerson, Irene, Vol. 3: 82–83
Enforcement Act, Vol. 2: 68, 72
Engel, George, Vol. 4: 47
England, Vol. 2: 96. *See also* Great Britain
English settlers, Vol. 1: 22–30, *24, 26*
Equal Rights Amendment (ERA), Vol. 5: 76, 76–86, 80, 84
Equality League of Self-Supporting Women, Vol. 4: 113
Ervin, Sam, Jr., Vol. 5: 83, 84
espionage, Vol. 5: 133
Europe, Vol. 2: 22–23
Evangelical Church Army, Vol. 4: *101*
Evans, Oliver, Vol. 4: 72
The Examiner—Defended in a Fair and Sober Answer (Williams), Vol. 1: 18
executive branch, Vol. 1: 125
Executive Order 9066, Vol. 5: 13, 19, 20–21
executive privilege, Vol. 2: 57
expansion, Vol. 3: 73–75
Ex parte Endo, Vol. 5: 17
external taxes, Vol. 1: 75

F
factions, Vol. 1: 133
farming, Vol. 2: 101, 103
FDIC. *See* Federal Deposit Insurance Corporation
Federal Bureau of Investigation (FBI), Vol. 5: 20, 25, 26–27, 31
Federal Deposit Insurance Corporation (FDIC), Vol. 4: 126
federal government, Vol. 1: 124
Federal Reserve Board, Vol. 4: 123
Federal Reserve System, Vol. 4: 123
The Federalist Papers (Madison, Hamilton, and Jay), Vol. 1: 126
Federalist Party
    Vol. 2:
        Alien and Sedition Acts and, 28–29
        criticism of Embargo Acts, 70–72
        election of 1800, 36–37
        opposition to Louisiana Purchase, 46–48
        opposition to War of 1812, 83–84
        overview of, 12
        Sedition Act and, 25
federalists, Vol. 1: 125–132
The Feminine Mystique (Friedan), Vol. 5: 77, 78
feminism, Vol. 5: 77–86
Ferdinand, Franz, Archduke of Austria, Vol. 4: 80
Ferguson, John, Vol. 4: 54, 55
Ferraro, Geraldine, Vol. 4: 120
fetus, Vol. 5: 62, 63, 67, 73–74

Field, David Dudley, Vol. 4: 18
Fielden, Samuel, Vol. 4: 44, 47
Fifteenth Amendment
    Vol. 3: 115, 116, *116,* 117–120
    Vol. 4: 53
Filene, Edward, Vol. 4: 129
filibustering, Vol. 3: 34
Finkbine, Sherri, Vol. 5: 65–66, 66
First Amendment
    Vol. 2: 26
    Vol. 4: 49
First Continental Congress, Vol. 1: 81, 87, 88–89, 92, 104
The First Great Awakening, Vol. 2: 115
First New Deal, Vol. 4: 126
Fischer, Adolph, Vol. 4: 47
Fiske, Robert, Vol. 5: 112
Florida
    Vol. 2: 45, 54
    Vol. 4: 17–18, 19, 20
    Vol. 5: 122–132
Florida Supreme Court, Vol. 5: 125, 127, 129, 131, 132
flywheel magneto, Vol. 4: 73
Folsom, Nathaniel, Vol. 1: 110
Force Bill, Vol. 2: 127–128
Ford, Gerald, Vol. 5: 108, 119–120
Ford, Henry, Vol. 4: *70,* 70–78, *71, 76,* 88
Ford Motor Company, Vol. 4: *70,* 70–78, 76
442nd Regimental Combat Team, Vol. 5: 17
"Fourteen Points" speech, Vol. 4: 90–91
Fourteenth Amendment
    Vol. 3: 114–120
    Vol. 4: 52–53, 56, 58, 111
    Vol. 5: 42, 45, 81, 82, 101, 104, 107–108, 110
France
    Vol. 1: 101
    Vol. 2: 22–23, 36, 43–44, 64, 74–75
    Vol. 4: 91
    Vol. 5: 48–49, 50
Frankfurter, Felix, Vol. 5: 19
Franklin, Benjamin, Vol. 1: 74, 94, 96, 96, 104–105, 108
Freedmen's Bureau, Vol. 3: 115
freedom of the press, Vol. 1: 52–58
Free-Soil Party, Vol. 3: 64
Frelinghuysen, Jacob, Vol. 1: 63
Frelinghuysen, Theodore, Vol. 3: 19, *19*
Frémont, John C., Vol. 3: *74*
French Indochina, Vol. 5: 49
French Revolution, Vol. 2: 12–13
Friedan, Betty, Vol. 5: 77, 78
Fronterio, Sharron, Vol. 5: 82
Fronterio v. Richardson, Vol. 5: 82
Fuchs, Klaus, Vol. 5: 29
fugitive
    Vol. 3: 133
    Vol. 4: 133
Fugitive Slave Law of 1850, Vol. 3: 65, 67–68

G
Gage, Thomas, Vol. 1: 80, 81, 82–83
Gaines, Lloyd, Vol. 5: 37–38
Gallatin, Albert, Vol. 2: 25–26, 27, 68
Galloway, Joseph, Vol. 1: 88–89, 90
Garrison, William Lloyd
    Vol. 2: 117, *118*
    Vol. 3: 53
Gary, Joseph, Vol. 4: 48
Geneva Accords, Vol. 5: 50
George III, King of England, Vol. 1: 70, 80, 81, 93, 95, 97
Georgia
    Vol. 2: 128
    Vol. 3: 12–13
German Americans, Vol. 5: 14
Germany, Vol. 4: 81–85, 86, 88, 91, 125
Gerry, Elbridge, Vol. 1: 126
Gilman, Nicholas, Vol. 1: 118
Ginsburg, Ruth Bader, Vol. 5: 107–108
gold, Vol. 3: 63
Goldwater, Barry, Vol. 5: 91, 97
Gompers, Samuel, Vol. 4: 27
Gonzalez, Henry, Vol. 5: 96
Good, Sarah, Vol. 1: 43, 44–45
Gore, Al
    Vol. 4: 20
    Vol. 5: 122–132
government
    Vol. 1:
        Articles of Confederation, 104–112
        Constitutional Convention, 113–122
        Constitution, ratification of, 124–131
gradualists, Vol. 2: 122
Grand Council, Vol. 1: 88–89
Grant, Ulysses S.
    Vol. 3: 125, 127
    Vol. 4: 13
Grantham, Thomas, Vol. 1: 36, 37
Gratz, Jennifer, Vol. 5: 103–104, *104,* 105
Gratz v. Bollinger, Vol. 5: 104, 105, 107
Great Awakening, Vol. 1: 60–68, 62, 64
Great Britain
    Vol. 1: 70–78, 80–90, 92–102
    Vol. 2: 13–14, 64–68, 74–76
    Vol. 3: 35, 48
    Vol. 4: 81–83, 85, 86, 88, 91. *See also* War of 1812
Great Compromise, Vol. 1: 122
Great Depression, Vol. 4: 108, 124–132
Great Strike of 1877, Vol. 4: 22–30, 24, 28
Green Party, Vol. 5: 124
Greene, Nathanael, Vol. 1: 97
Grenville, George, Vol. 1: 70–71, 76

Grimes, James, Vol. 3: 132
Grimké, Sarah, Vol. 3: 57
Grinnell, Julius, Vol. 4: 47, 48, 49
Griswold v. Connecticut, Vol. 5: 71
Grutter, Barbara, Vol. 5: *104*,
    104–105, 110
Grutter v. Bollinger,
    Vol. 5: 104–105, 110
Gulf of Tonkin, Vol. 5: 53
Gurin, Patricia, Vol. 5: 106

H
Hall, Fawn, Vol. 5: 97
Hamacher, Patrick, Vol. 5:
    103–104, *104*
Hamilton, Alexander
    Vol. 1:
        Articles of Confederation
            and, 115
        as Federalist leader, 32
        The Federalist Papers, 126
        life of, 116
        ratification of
            Constitution and, 127,
            130–131
    Vol. 2:
        duel with Aaron Burr, 53
        during elections of 1800,
            36–37
        Federalist Party and, 12
        Jay's Treaty and, 16,
            18–20
        portrait of, *19, 32,* 53
Hamilton, Andrew, Vol. 1: 54, 55,
    56–58, *57*
Hancock, John, Vol. 1: 83
Harding, Warren, Vol. 4: 96, 122
Harlan, John Marshall, Vol. 4: 57
Harper's Weekly magazine
    Vol. 3: 128
    Vol. 4: 30, 40
Harris, Katherine,
    Vol. 5: 124–125, 126, 128
Harrison, William Henry,
    Vol. 2: 77, 79
Hawaii, Vol. 5: 12, 13, 14
Hawley, Joseph, Vol. 4: 39
Hayes, George E.C., Vol. 5: 38
Hayes, Rutherford B.
    Vol. 4:
        Chinese Exclusion Act
            and, 35
        election of 1876 and, *13,*
            13–20
        Great Strike of 1877 and,
            25, 26, 29
    Vol. 5: 126
Haymarket Affair, Vol. 4: 42–50,
    45, 46
Haymarket Monument, Vol. 4: 50
"healing witches," Vol. 1: 42
Hearst, William Randolph,
    Vol. 4: 60
Henry, Patrick, Vol. 1: 75, 87
Herrick, Robert, Vol. 4: 87
Hirabayashi, Gordon,
    Vol. 5: 16–17, 18
Hiss, Alger, Vol. 5: 26, *28,* 28
Hobson, Richard,
    Vol. 4: 102, 106
Ho Chi Minh, Vol. 5: 48, 49

Hollywood, Vol. 5: 25
Honduras, Vol. 5: 90
Hook, Sidney, Vol. 5: 32–33
Hoover, Herbert, Vol. 4: 122,
    124–125, 129, *132*
Hoover, J. Edgar, Vol. 5: 31
House Judiciary Committee,
    Vol. 5: 116, 118
House of Representatives. See
    U.S. House of Representatives
House Un-American Activities
    Committee (HUAC),
    Vol. 5: 25–26, 28, 31
Houston, Charles, Vol. 5: 37
Houston, Sam, Vol. 3: 32, 33, *33*
Howells, William Dean, Vol. 4: 49
HUAC. See House Un-American
    Activities Committee
Hubbard, Elizabeth, Vol. 1: 43
Hutchinson, Anne, Vol. 1: 14, *15*
Hutchinson, Thomas, Vol. 1: 73

I
Illinois, Vol. 5: 131
immigrants, Vol. 4: 112
immigration
    Vol. 4: 32–40, *33, 37, 38*
    Vol. 5: 12
impeachment
    Vol. 3: 122–132, *127, 129,*
        130, 131
    Vol. 5: 96, 112–120,
        115, 117
imperialism, Vol. 4: 64–68
impressment, Vol. 2: 17, 65–66
inauguration
    Vol. 3: 133
    Vol. 4: 133
independence. See Declaration of
    Independence
Indian Removal Act,
    Vol. 3: 12–20
induced abortion, Vol. 5: 63
industrial policies of Henry Ford,
    Vol. 4: 70, 70–78, *71, 76*
industry, Vol. 2: 96–104, 124
Inglis, Charles, Vol. 1: 101
interchangeable parts,
    Vol. 4: 72, 73
interest rates, Vol. 4: 123
intern, Vol. 5: 133
internal tax, Vol. 1: 75
internment of Japanese
    Americans, Vol. 5: 12–22,
    13, 15, 21
Iran, Vol. 5: 92–93, 94
Iran-Contra affair,
    Vol. 5: 88–98, *90, 92, 96*
Irreconcilables, Vol. 4: 95
isolationism, Vol. 4: 95.
    See also neutrality, American
Israel, Vol. 5: 93
Issei (first generation), Vol. 5: 12
Italian Americans, Vol. 5: 14

J
Jackson, Andrew
    Vol. 2:
        elections of 1824 and,
            107, 108–109
        Indian removal and, 128

    nullification and, 127,
        131–132
    Vol. 3:
        BUS and, 22–27
        Indian removal and,
            17–18, 20
        Indian Removal Act and,
            13–14
        portrait of, *26*
        Texas annexation and, 34
Jackson, Robert, Vol. 5: 21
Jamestown (VA), Vol. 1: 34, 35, *36*
Japanese Americans, internment
    of, Vol. 5: 12–22, *13, 15, 21*
Jay, John
    Vol. 1: 117, 126, 132, *132*
    Vol. 2: 14–15, *17,* 18
Jay's Treaty, Vol. 2: 14–20
Jefferson, Thomas
    Vol. 1:
        Aaron Burr and, 52
        Declaration of
            Independence and, 8,
            94–95, *96,* 97
        as Democratic-
            Republican leader,
            32–33
        ratification of
            Constitution and, 128
        writer of "Declaration of
            the Causes and
            Necessity of Taking Up
            Arms," 92
    Vol. 2:
        Burr Conspiracy and, 56
        Democratic-Republican
            Party and, 12
        elections of 1800 and,
            35–36, 38–40
        Embargo Acts and, 66–70
        expansion and, 42
        on Louisiana, 44
        Louisiana Purchase and,
            45, 49–50
        portrait of, *19, 40*
    Vol. 4: 8
    Vol. 5: 8
Jeffreys, Herbert, Vol. 1: 39
Jenyns, Soame, Vol. 1: 78
Jews, Vol. 1: 60
"Jim Crow" laws
    Vol. 4: 53–54, *54,* 55
    Vol. 5: 36
Johnson, Andrew
    Vol. 3:
        civil rights and, 112–120
        impeachment of, 8,
            122–132, *127, 129,*
            130, 131
        Thirteenth Amendment
            and, 104
    Vol. 5: 116
Johnson, Hiram, Vol. 4: 95
Johnson, Lyndon B., Vol. 5:
    50–53, 56, 58, 60
Jones, Paula, Vol. 5: 112–113, 114
Jordan, Vernon, Vol. 5: 113
Journal (New York newspaper),
    Vol. 4: 60
Joyce, Charles, Vol. 4: 39
judicial branch, Vol. 1: 125

jury nullification, Vol. 1: 57, 58

K
Kansas, Vol. 3: 73, 75–76, 77
Kansas-Nebraska Act, Vol. 3: 72–80, 74
Kearney, Dennis, Vol. 4: 38
Kendall, David, Vol. 5: 115, 120
Kennedy, John F., Vol. 5: 49–50, 100
Kennedy, Robert F., Vol. 5: 60
Kentucky, Vol. 2: 27
Kentucky Resolutions, Vol. 2: 72, 130
Kerry, John, Vol. 5: 98
Khomeini, Ruhollah, Vol. 5: 92–93
King, Martin Luther, Jr., Vol. 5: 59
King Philip's War, Vol. 1: 22–30, 24
King, Rufus, Vol. 2: 91, 92, 93
Kissinger, Henry, Vol. 5: 54, 55
Klann, William, Vol. 4: 77
Knox, Henry, Vol. 2: 19
Kohut, Andrew, Vol. 5: 117
Korean War, Vol. 5: 48, 49
Korematsu, Fred, Vol. 5: 18, 21
Korematsu v. United States, Vol. 5: 17, 18, 19, 21, 22
Kristol, William, Vol. 5: 131

L
labor movement
    Vol. 4:
        Great Strike of 1877, 22–30
        Haymarket Affair, 42–50, 45, 46
labor unions. See unions
La Follette, Robert, Vol. 4: 88
laissez-faire policies, Vol. 4: 128
land, Vol. 1: 27–30, 110–111
Laos, Vol. 5: 50, 53
Latin America, Vol. 4: 80
latitude
    Vol. 3: 133
    Vol. 4: 133
Lawson, Deodat, Vol. 1: 47
LDF. See Legal Defense Fund
League to Enforce Peace (LEP), Vol. 4: 98
League of Nations, Vol. 4: 8, 89–98, 92, 97
Lebanon, Vol. 5: 93, 94
Le Duc Tho, Vol. 5: 54
Lee, Richard Henry, Vol. 1: 94, 105
Legal Defense Fund (LDF), Vol. 5: 36, 37
legislative branch, Vol. 1: 125
legislature, Vol. 1: 133
Lenin, Vladimir, Vol. 5: 24, 33
Leonard, Daniel, Vol. 1: 89
LEP. See League to Enforce Peace
Lewinsky, Monica, Vol. 5: 113–120
Lexington (MA), Vol. 1: 83–84, 89
liberal, Vol. 5: 133
The Liberator, Vol. 2: 117
Lincoln, Abraham
    Vol. 3:
        freeing of the slaves and, 102–110

murder of, 122
photograph of, 97
portrait of, 105
Reconstruction and, 112
response to Dred Scott case, 90
secession of Southern states and, 93–100, 94
    Vol. 4: 12
Lincoln's Legal Loyal League, Vol. 3: 106
Lingg, Louis, Vol. 4: 47
Livingston, Edward, Vol. 2: 26
Livingston, Robert
    Vol. 1: 94, 96, 102
    Vol. 2: 16
Lodge, Henry Cabot, Vol. 4: 65, 66, 95–96
Long, Huey, Vol. 4: 131
Louisiana, Vol. 2: 43–44
Louisiana Purchase, Vol. 2: 42–50
Louisiana Territory, Vol. 2: 42
Love, Ken, Vol. 5: 59
Lowell, Francis Cabot, Vol. 2: 97, 98, 99
Lowell (MA), Vol. 2: 99–100
Lowell System, Vol. 2: 97–99
Loyalists, Vol. 1: 90
Lum, Dyer, Vol. 4: 49
Lusitania, Vol. 4: 85, 86, 86
Lynch, Thomas, Jr., Vol. 1: 110

M
Madison, James
    Vol. 1: 117–121, 121, 126, 128, 131
    Vol. 2: 16, 18, 69, 76, 78–81, 130, 131
Maine
    Vol. 2: 88
    Vol. 3: 62
Manhattan Project, Vol. 5: 29
Manifest Destiny
    Vol. 3: 42–43, 46–47
    Vol. 4: 64–65
Marshall, George, Vol. 5: 29
Marshall, John, Vol. 2: 37, 56–58, 59
Marshall, Thurgood, Vol. 5: 37, 38, 38–46
Martin, Luther, Vol. 2: 57
Marx, Karl
    Vol. 4: 28, 42, 43
    Vol. 5: 24, 25
Marxist Leninism, Vol. 5: 24
Maryland, Vol. 1: 106, 111
Mason, George, Vol. 1: 125
mass production, Vol. 4: 71–73, 74–75, 77, 122
Massachusetts, Vol. 1: 42–50, 46, 48, 80–90, 116
Massasoit. See Usamequin (Massasoit)
Mather, Cotton, Vol. 1: 19, 30, 48, 48–49
McCarthy, Joseph, Vol. 5: 29–34, 30
McCarthyism, Vol. 5: 30–34
McCorvey, Norma, Vol. 5: 66–67, 68, 68
McDuffie, George, Vol. 2: 122
McFarlane, Robert, Vol. 5: 93, 94

McKean, Thomas, Vol. 2: 39
McKinley, William, Vol. 4: 61, 61–62
McLaurin, George, Vol. 5: 38
McLaurin v. Oklahoma State Regents, Vol. 5: 38
McLean, John, Vol. 3: 89
Metacomet (King Philip), Vol. 1: 23–30
Methodism, Vol. 2: 115
Mexican War, Vol. 3: 42–50, 45
Mexico
    Vol. 2: 54–55
    Vol. 3: 32–34, 42–50
    Vol. 4: 82
militia, Vol. 1: 133
minorities. See affirmative action; African Americans; Japanese Americans, internment of
Minutemen, Vol. 1: 81, 82, 83–84, 84
miscarriage, Vol. 5: 63
Mississippi, Vol. 3: 102, 106, 108, 114
Mississippi River, Vol. 2: 42
Missouri, Vol. 3: 62, 75, 82, 84
Missouri Compromise
    Vol. 2: 86–94
    Vol. 3: 72, 73, 78
Model T, Vol. 4: 70, 71, 72, 75, 76
Mondale, Walter, Vol. 4: 120
Monroe Doctrine, Vol. 4: 80, 95, 98
Monroe, James
    Vol. 2: 89, 106
    Vol. 4: 80, 95
Morris, Gouverneur, Vol. 1: 58
Morris, Lewis, Vol. 1: 53–54
Mott, Lucretia
    Vol. 3: 54, 55
    Vol. 4: 110
Murphy, Frank, Vol. 5: 21, 22
Murray, Judith Sargent Stevens, Vol. 3: 52
Myrdal, Gunnar, Vol. 5: 43

N
NAACP. See National Association for the Advancement of Colored People
Nabrit, James M., Vol. 5: 38
Nader, Ralph, Vol. 5: 124
NARAL. See National Association for the Reform of Abortion Laws
Narragansett, Vol. 1: 22, 26, 29
National American Woman Suffrage Association (NAWSA), Vol. 4: 112, 113
National Association for the Advancement of Colored People (NAACP), Vol. 5: 36–38, 39
National Association for the Reform of Abortion Laws (NARAL), Vol. 5: 71
National Labor Union (NLU), Vol. 4: 23
National Organization for Women (NOW), Vol. 5: 78–81, 80

National Right to Life
 Committee, Vol. 5: 69
National Security Council
 (NSC), Vol. 5: 91, 93
National Woman Suffrage
 Association (NWSA), Vol. 4:
 110, 112
National Woman's Party (NWP),
 Vol. 4: 113–114, *114, 117*
Native Americans
  Vol. 1: 14, 16, 22–30, *24,
   26,* 32–40
  Vol. 3: 12–20
naturalization
  Vol. 3: 133
  Vol. 4: 133
Naturalization Act, Vol. 2: 24, 26
navy, Vol. 2: 78
NAWSA. *See* National American
 Woman Suffrage Association
Nebraska, Vol. 3: 73
Nebraska Association Opposed to
 Woman Suffrage, Vol. 4: 120
Neebe, Oscar, Vol. 4: 47
neutrality, American,
 Vol. 4: 81, 87
New Deal, Vol. 4: 122–132,
 127, 132
New England, Vol. 2: 83–84,
 97–98
New Jersey, Vol. 3: 58
New Jersey Plan, Vol. 1: 120–122
"New Lights," Vol. 1: 65–68
New Mexico
  Vol. 3: 64
  Vol. 5: 122
New Orleans (LA),
 Vol. 2: 42, 44–45
New York
  Vol. 1: 52–58
  Vol. 5: 64
New York Gazette, Vol. 1: 53
New York Times, Vol. 4: 29
New York Weekly Journal,
 Vol. 1: 53–54
Newton, Isaac, Vol. 1: 61
Nicaragua, Vol. 5: 89, 90–91
1950 Internal Security Act,
 Vol. 5: 33
Nineteenth Amendment
  Vol. 4: 110–120, *114, 117*
  Vol. 5: 76, 76, 77
Nisei (second generation),
  Vol. 5: 12, 20–21
Nixon, Richard
  Vol. 3: 126
  Vol. 5: Equal Rights
   Amendment and, 79
   Vietnam War and, 53–54,
    55, 57, 60
   Watergate, 89, 96, 116
NLU. *See* National Labor Union
The North, Vol. 2: 90–93
North Korea, Vol. 5: 29, 48
North Vietnam, Vol. 5: 49–60
North, Lord, Vol. 1: 82
North, Oliver, Vol. 5: 91–92, 92,
 93, 94–95, 97, 98
Northwest Ordinance, Vol. 2: 87

NOW. *See* National Organization
 for Women
NSC. *See* National Security
 Council
Nullification Crisis,
 Vol. 2: 124–132
NWP. *See* National
 Woman's Party
NWSA. *See* National Woman
 Suffrage Association

O
obiter dictum, Vol. 3: 89
O'Connor, Sandra Day,
 Vol. 5: 107
"Old Ironsides," Vol. 2: 78
"Old Lights," Vol. 1: 65–68
Oliver, Andrew, Vol. 1: 72
Olson, Culbert, Vol. 5: 19
Operation Rescue, Vol. 5: 69
Oregon
  Vol. 4: 15
  Vol. 5: 122
Osborne, Sarah, Vol. 1: 43, 44–45
Otis, James, Vol. 1: 76

P
Paine, Thomas
  Vol. 1: 97–98, 99, 101
  Vol. 2: 48–49
Palm Beach County (FL),
 Vol. 5: 128, 129
Panama Canal, Vol. 4: 80
Parker, John, Vol. 1: 83–84
Parliament
  Vol. 1:
   American Revolution
    and, 82, 90
   Coercive Acts passed
    by, 80
   Prohibitory Act, 94
   Stamp Act crisis and, 70,
    71, 73–78
Parris, Samuel, Vol. 1: 43, 44, 47
Parsons, Albert, Vol. 4: 44, 47, 50
Parsons, Lucy, Vol. 4: 50
Paterson, William, Vol. 1: 120
Patriots, Vol. 1: 80–90
Paul, Alice
  Vol. 4: 113, 115, *117*
  Vol. 5: 76, 76
Pearl Harbor (HI), Vol. 5: 13
Pennsylvania Railroad,
 Vol. 4: 25, 26
"Pentagon Papers," Vol. 5: 60
perjury, Vol. 5: 115, 117
Perot, Ross, Vol. 5: 112
Pershing, John "Black Jack,"
 Vol. 4: 82–83, 83
petition
  Vol. 1: 133
  Vol. 3: 133
  Vol. 4: 133
Philadelphia (PA), Vol. 1: 92
Philippines, Vol. 4: 63, 64, 65, 66,
 67–68
Phips, Mary, Vol. 1: 46
Phips, William, Vol. 1: 45, 46–47
Pickering, Timothy, Vol. 2: 71, 71
Pierce, Franklin, Vol. 3: 73
pietism, Vol. 1: 61, 63, 68, 133

Pilgrims
  Vol. 1:
   King Philip's War and,
    22–30, *24, 26*
   Roger Williams and,
    12–13, 17
Pitt, William, Vol. 1: 90
Pittsburgh (PA) strike, Vol. 4: 25
plantation
  Vol. 1: 133
  Vol. 3: 133
  Vol. 4: 133
Plessy, Homer, Vol. 4: 54–58
Plessy v. Ferguson
  Vol. 4: *52,* 52–58, *54*
  Vol. 5: 36, 40, 44, 67
Plymouth (MA), Vol. 1: 13
Poindexter, John, Vol. 5: 94–95, 97
political parties, Vol. 2: 12
politics
  Vol. 2: 74–75, 91
  Vol. 3: 28, 59–60
Polk, James K.
  Vol. 3:
   Mexican War and, 46–47
   Mexico and, 42–43, 49
   Texas annexation and, 35
   Whig Party and, 48
polls
  Vol. 3: 133
  Vol. 4: 133
Poor Richard's Almanac (Franklin),
  Vol. 1: 74
popular vote
  Vol. 4: 14–15
  Vol. 5: 123
Powell, Lewis, Vol. 5: 102, 105, 106
Praying Indians, Vol. 1: 25
pregnancy. *See* abortion
prejudice, Vol. 4: 34–40.
  See also racism
preparedness program, Vol. 4: 81,
 82, 84–85, 87–88, 102
Presbyterians, Vol. 1: 60
Prescott, Samuel, Vol. 1: 83
presidential election of 2000, Vol.
 5: 122–132, *123, 128, 130*
press, freedom of, Vol. 1: 52–58
privacy, right to, Vol. 5: 71, 74
Proctor, John, Vol. 1: 45
progressives, Vol. 4: 87–88
Prohibition, Vol. 4: 100–108,
 101, 106
Prohibition Party, Vol. 4: 101
Prohibitory Act, Vol. 1: 94
propaganda, Vol. 5: 133
Protestantism, Vol. 1: 60, 61–68
Providence (RI), Vol. 1: 14
public schools. *See* schools
Pulitzer, Joseph, Vol. 4: 60
Puritans
  Vol. 1:
   Native Americans and,
    27, 29–30
   Pilgrims and, 23
   Roger Williams and,
    12–20, *15, 19*
   Salem witch trials, 42–50,
    46, 48
Putnam, Ann, Vol. 1: 43, 45, 47
Pym, William, Vol. 1: 77

Q

Quakers
 Vol. 2: 115
 Vol. 3: 52
 Vol. 4: 115
quickening, Vol. 5: 62, 63
quotas, Vol. 5: 101–102, 104

R

race. *See* affirmative action;
 African Americans; *Brown v.*
 Board of Education
racism
 Vol. 4: 39, 65, 67, 112
 Vol. 5: 12
Radical Republicans
 Vol. 3: 112–113, 115–118,
 119, 123–132
 Vol. 4: 13
railroads, Vol. 4: 32, 33, 33
railroad strike of 1877, Vol. 4:
 22–30, 24, 28
railroad unions, Vol. 4: 23–25
Randolph, Edmund, Vol. 2: 19
Ray, Robert, Vol. 5: 118
Reagan, Ronald, Vol. 5: 18,
 88–98, 96
recession, Vol. 3: 22
Reconstruction
 Vol. 3: 112–113, 118–120,
 122–132
 Vol. 4: 12, 13–14, 17, 52,
 52–53
Reconstruction Finance
 Corporation (RFC),
 Vol. 4: 124–125
recounts (2000 national election),
 Vol. 5: 124–132, 128
Red Scare, Vol. 5: 25
Regents of the University of
 California v. Bakke,
 Vol. 5: 101, 101–102
Rehnquist, William, Vol. 5: 109
religion
 Vol. 1: 12–20, 42–50,
 60–68, 62, 64
 Vol. 2: 115, 118–121
 Vol. 3: 49, 57, 59–60
Republican Party
 Vol. 3:
  birth of, 74
  civil rights and, 112–113,
  116–120
  in election of 1860,
  93–94
  emancipation and,
  106–107
  impeachment of Andrew
  Johnson and, 122–132
  Thirteenth Amendment
  and, 109
 Vol. 4: 12–20, 36, 93–94
 Vol. 5: 112, 113, 116, 117,
 122–132
Reservationists, Vol. 4: 93, 94, 95
Revere, Paul, Vol. 1: 83, 89
reverse discrimination,
 Vol. 5: 102, 104–105
revival, Vol. 1: 63–65, 133
RFC. *See* Reconstruction
 Finance Corporation

Rhode Island,
 Vol. 1: 14, 15, 17, 117
Rhode Island's Electoral College,
 Vol. 5: 123
right to privacy, Vol. 5: 71, 74
Robertson, Pat, Vol. 5: 97
Rockingham, Lord, Vol. 1: 73
Roe v. Wade,
 Vol. 5: 66–74, 68, 70
Roman Catholic Church, Vol. 5:
 69, 73–74
Roosevelt, Eleanor, Vol. 5: 22
Roosevelt, Franklin
 Vol. 4: 81, 104, 125–132
 Vol. 5: 13–14, 17, 19, 20–21,
 22, 28
Roosevelt, Theodore,
 Vol. 4: 63, 63
Ross, John, Vol. 3: 14–15, 20
Rough Riders, Vol. 4: 63, 63
Ruff, Charles, Vol. 5: 115,
 119–120
Rutledge, James, Vol. 1: 102

S

sabotage, Vol. 5: 133
Saints, Vol. 1: 23
Salem (MA), Vol. 1: 13
Salem witch trials, Vol. 1: 42–50,
 46, 48
saloons, Vol. 4: 105, 107
Sandinistas, Vol. 5: 89, 90, 94
San Francisco (CA), Vol. 4:
 32–33, 34
San Francisco Chronicle, Vol. 5: 20
Santa Anna, Antonio López de,
 Vol. 3: 32, 33
Santiago (Cuba), Vol. 4: 63
Sassamon, Vol. 1: 25
Saudi Arabia, Vol. 5: 91
Scalia, Antonin, Vol. 5: 109
Schlafly, Phyllis, Vol. 5: 84,
 84–86
Schmitz, John G., Vol. 5: 86
schools
 Vol. 5:
  affirmative action in
  public universities,
  100–110, 101, 103,
  104, 107
  Brown v. Board of
  Education, 36–46,
  38, 44
Schroeder, Patricia, Vol. 5: 82
Schurz, Carl, Vol. 4: 66–67, 68
Schwab, Michael, Vol. 4: 47
science, Vol. 1: 61
Scott, Dred, Vol. 3: 82–90, 83
Scott, Melinda, Vol. 4: 116
Scott, Thomas, Vol. 4: 26, 29
SDS. *See* Students for a
 Democratic Society
secession of Southern states,
 Vol. 3: 92, 92–100, 94, 97
Second Continental Congress,
 Vol. 1: 92–93, 104
The Second Great Awakening
 Vol. 2: 115–116
 Vol. 3: 52–53
Second New Deal, Vol. 4: 126
second women's movement,
 Vol. 5: 77–78

SEC. *See* Security and
 Exchange Commission
sectionalism, Vol. 2: 91
Security and Exchange
 Commission (SEC), Vol. 4: 126
Sedition Act, Vol. 2: 25. *See also*
 Alien and Sedition Acts
seditious libel, Vol. 1: 52, 54–58
segregation
 Vol. 4: 52, 52–58, 54
 Vol. 5: 36–46, 38, 44, 100
Seminole, Vol. 3: 15
Senate. *See* U.S. Senate
Seneca Falls Convention, Vol. 3:
 52–60, 55, 56
Sensenbrenner, James, Vol. 5: 118
separation of church and state,
 Vol. 1: 12–20, 15, 19
Separatists, Vol. 1: 12–13, 17, 23
Serbia, Vol. 4: 80
Seward, William, Vol. 3: 122
sexual rights, Vol. 5: 77
Shays, Daniel, Vol. 1: 116
Sheean, Vincent, Vol. 4: 124
Sherman, John, Vol. 4: 20
Sherman, Roger,
 Vol. 1: 94, 96, 119, 122
Shouse, Jarrett, Vol. 4: 130
Sickles, Daniel, Vol. 4: 15
Sims, Thomas, Vol. 3: 65
Six Companies, Vol. 4: 32, 35
skirmishes, Vol. 1: 133
Slater, Samuel, Vol. 2: 96
slavery
 Vol. 1:
  Declaration of
  Independence and, 95
  taxation and, 109–110
 Vol. 2:
  depiction of
  slave market, 120
  Missouri Compromise
  and, 86–94
  slave owners and aboli-
  tionism, 121–122
  slave trade, 86
  tariffs and, 130
 Vol. 3:
  in California/New
  Mexico, 62
  freeing of the slaves,
  102–110, 105, 108
  Mexican War and, 47
  secession of Southern
  states and, 92, 92–100,
  94, 97
  in Texas, 35
  Texas annexation and,
  37–38, 39. *See also*
  abolitionists
Smith Act of 1940, Vol. 5: 32
Smith, William, Vol. 1: 101
Smoot-Hawley Tariff, Vol. 4: 125
smuggling
 Vol. 1: 70–71
 Vol. 2: 68
socialism
 Vol. 4: 42–43, 87, 120, 128
 Vol. 5: 31
Social Security, Vol. 4: 126
Society of Friends. *See* Quakers

The South, Vol. 2: 93–94
South Carolina
    Vol. 2: 127, 130
    Vol. 3: 95, 97–98
South Carolina Exposition and
    Protest of 1828, Vol. 2: 131
South Korea, Vol. 5: 29, 48
South Vietnam, Vol. 5: 49–60
Southern states
    Vol. 3:
        civil rights for African
            Americans and, 113,
            114, 115–116,
            117–120
        freeing of the slaves and,
            102–110
        secession of, 92, 92–100,
            94, 97
sovereignty
    Vol. 1: 133
    Vol. 3: 77
Soviet Union
    Vol. 5:
        Cold War anti-
            Communism and,
            24–34
        Iran-Contra affair and,
            88–89
        Vietnam War and, 48, 54,
            55–56
Spain
    Vol. 2: 43–44, 54
    Vol. 3: 32
Spanish-American War, Vol. 4:
    60–68, 61, 63
Spies, August, Vol. 4: 44, 47
spontaneous abortion, Vol. 5: 63
Stalin, Joseph, Vol. 5: 24
Stamp Act Congress, Vol. 1: 73,
    76
Stamp Act Crisis,
    Vol. 1: 70–78, 72, 77
Stanton, Edwin,
    Vol. 3: 125, 127, 127, 128
    Vol. 5: 116
Stanton, Elizabeth Cady
    Vol. 3: 54–55, 56, 57, 58, 119
    Vol. 4: 110
Starr, Kenneth, Vol. 5: 112–113,
    114, 115, 118
steam engine, Vol. 2: 96
Stevens, John Paul, Vol. 5: 130
Stevens, Thaddeus, Vol. 3: 112,
    112–113, 117, 118, 120
stock market, Vol. 4: 126
stock market crash, Vol. 4: 123–124
stocks, Vol. 4: 122
Stoddard, Solomon, Vol. 1: 62
STOP ERA, Vol. 5: 84–85, 86
Stowe, Harriet Beecher, Vol. 2: 121
Strader v. Graham, Vol. 3: 86
Strangers, Vol. 1: 23
Strike of 1877,
    Vol. 4: 22–30, 24, 28
strikes, textile mill, Vol. 2: 99
Strong, Josiah, Vol. 4: 65
Students for a Democratic Society
    (SDS), Vol. 5: 58
submarines, Vol. 4: 81
Suffolk Resolves, Vol. 1: 89

suffrage
    Vol. 3: 115–120, 116
    Vol. 4: 110–120, 114, 117.
        See also Seneca Falls
        Convention
Sugar Act, Vol. 1: 70–71
Sumner, Charles,
    Vol. 3: 50, 129, 129
Sumner, William, Vol. 3:
    108–109, 112
Supreme Court. See U.S. Supreme
    Court
Susquehannock natives, Vol. 1:
    32, 33, 38
Sweatt v. Painter, Vol. 5: 38
Sweitzer, Donal R., Vol. 5: 123

T
Taft, William Howard, Vol. 4: 85,
    98, 102
Talmadge, Herman, Vol. 5: 46
Taney, Roger Brooke, Vol. 3:
    86–87
tariffs
    Vol. 2: 124–128, 126
    Vol. 4: 125
taxation, Vol. 1: 32–40, 70–78,
    109–110
Taylor, Stuart, Jr., Vol. 5: 132
Taylor, Zachary, Vol. 3: 43, 44, 45
Tecumseh, Vol. 2: 76, 77
Tell, David, Vol. 5: 131
temperance movement
    Vol. 3: 52
    Vol. 4: 100–101
Tennant, Gilbert, Vol. 1: 63, 65,
    67
Tennant, William, Vol. 1: 63, 65
Tenure of Office Act, Vol. 3: 124,
    125–127, 128, 130–132
territories, Vol. 3: 62–64
Tet Offensive, Vol. 5: 52
Texas
    Vol. 3: 32–40
    Vol. 5: 66–67
textile mills, Vol. 2: 97–104
therapeutic abortion exceptions,
    Vol. 5: 64, 65–66, 69
Thirteenth Amendment
    Vol. 3: 104, 108,
        108–110, 112
    Vol. 4: 52, 56, 57, 58
Thomas, Clarence, Vol. 5: 110
Thomas, Lorenzo, Vol. 3: 125
Tilden, Samuel
    Vol. 4: 14–15, 17–20
    Vol. 5: 126
Tisquantum, Vol. 1: 22
Tituba, Vol. 1: 43, 44, 45
tobacco, Vol. 1: 32
Toombs, Robert, Vol. 3: 64
Topeka (KS), Vol. 5: 39
totalitarian government, Vol. 5:
    55–56
Tourgée, Albion, Vol. 4: 54, 56
Trail of Tears, Vol. 3: 15
treason
    Vol. 1: 133
    Vol. 2: 56, 57–58

treaties
    Vol. 2: 79–80
    Vol. 3: 17–18, 45–46
Treaty of Guadeloupe-Hidalgo,
    Vol. 3: 45–46
Treaty of Paris, Vol. 1: 115
Treaty of Versailles, Vol. 4: 91, 92,
    94, 97
Triple Alliance (the Central
    Powers), Vol. 4: 80, 81, 90
Triple Entente (Allies), Vol. 4:
    80, 83, 84–85, 90, 91
Tripp, Linda, Vol. 5: 113, 114
Truman, Harry
    Vol. 5:
        Cold War
            anti-communism and,
            24, 25, 29, 33–34
        segregation and, 39
        Vietnam and, 48–49
Truth, Sojourner, Vol. 3: 57
Tule Lake internment camp
    (CA), Vol. 5: 16
"Twelve Reasons Why Women
    Should Vote" (National
    Woman Suffrage Publishing
    Company), Vol. 4: 118
Twenty-first Amendment,
    Vol. 4: 104
Tyler, John
    Vol. 2: 128
    Vol. 3: 34–36
tyranny
    Vol. 1: 133
    Vol. 3: 133
    Vol. 4: 133

U
UCD. See University of
    California at Davis
UN. See United Nations
Uncle Tom's Cabin (Stowe),
    Vol. 2: 121
Underwood, Oscar, Vol. 4: 107
unions
    Vol. 2: 99
    Vol. 4: 23–25, 28, 30,
        42–50, 45, 46, 108
    Vol. 5: 25
United Nations (UN)
    Vol. 4: 94
    Vol. 5: 29
universities, affirmative action in,
    Vol. 5: 100–110, 101, 103,
    104, 107
University of California at Davis
    (UCD), Vol. 5: 100–102, 103
University of Michigan, Vol. 5:
    103–110, 104, 107
Usamequin (Massasoit),
    Vol. 1: 22–23, 24, 27
U.S. Army
    Vol. 2: 78
    Vol. 5: 31
U.S. battleship Maine,
    Vol. 4: 61, 62
U.S. Commission on Civil Rights,
    Vol. 5: 129

U.S. Congress
    Vol. 1: 107–111, 114,
        115–116
    Vol. 2: 81, 83, 86–89
    Vol. 3: 18–20, 40, 103, 104,
        108–110, 113–116,
        125–126, 128,
        130–131
    Vol. 4: 16, 16–20
    Vol. 5: 26, 46, 76, 77,
        78–79, 81, 83–84, 88,
        90, 90–91, 95–96,
        115–117
U.S. House of Representatives
    Vol. 1: 124
    Vol. 2: 35–36
    Vol. 3: 108, 109, 125, 128
    Vol. 5: 115–117
U.S. Senate
    Vol. 3: 125–126, 128,
        131–132
    Vol. 4: 93–94, 96
    Vol. 5: 116, 117, 118, 120
U.S. Supreme Court
    Vol. 1: 53
    Vol. 2: 58
    Vol. 3: 86, 88–89
    Vol. 4:
        on Civil Rights Act of
            1875, 53
        Plessy v. Ferguson, 54,
            55–58
    Vol. 5:
        affirmative action and,
            101, 101–102,
            103–106, 108–110
        Brown v. Board of
            Education, 39–46
        Cold War
            anti-communism
            and, 32, 34
        election of 2000 and,
            125, 127, 129, 130,
            130, 131
        Equal Rights Amendment
            and, 81–82
        Korematsu v. United
            States, 17, 19, 21
        Paula Jones's case and,
            114
        Roe v. Wade, 67, 69, 71, 72
        segregation and, 36,
            37–38
        Utah, Vol. 4: 111
USS Chesapeake, Vol. 2: 65–66, 67
USS Constitution, Vol. 2: 78
USS Maddox, Vol. 5: 53

V
Valley Spirit (newspaper),
    Vol. 3: 107, 110
Van Buren, Martin, Vol. 3: 17, 34
Van Dam, Rip, Vol. 1: 52–53
Venona Project, Vol. 5: 26–27, 28
veto, Vol. 3: 28–29
Viet Cong, Vol. 5: 49–50, 51, 53
Vietnam War,
    Vol. 5: 48–60, 51, 52, 59
Vietnamization, Vol. 5: 53–54, 57

Villa, Pancho, Vol. 4: 82, 83
Villard, Oswald Garrison, Vol. 4: 88
Vinson, Fred, Vol. 5: 32
Virginia
    Vol. 1: 32–40, 106
    Vol. 2: 27
Virginia Plan, Vol. 1: 119–120
Volstead Act, Vol. 4: 103, 104
vote
    Vol. 1: 108–109
    Vol. 3: 115–120, 116
    Vol. 4: 105, 110–120,
        114, 117
    Vol. 5: 76, 76, 77, 122–132

W
Wade, Henry, Vol. 5: 66
wages, Vol. 4: 73–74, 75, 76, 77–78
Walker, David, Vol. 2: 116
Walker, Robert, Vol. 3: 37–38
Wall Street Journal, Vol. 4: 78
Wallace, Lew, Vol. 4: 19
Walsh, Lawrence, Vol. 5: 94–95, 96
Wampanoag, Vol. 1: 22–30
Wamsutta, Vol. 1: 23
War Hawks, Vol. 2: 81–82
War of 1812
    Vol. 2: 74–84
    Vol. 3: 92
Waring, J. Waties, Vol. 5: 39
Warren, Earl, Vol. 5: 40–41, 43
Warren, Joseph, Vol. 1: 83
Washington, George
    Vol. 1: 92, 98, 117, 118
    Vol. 2: 19
    Vol. 4: 100
Washington, John, Vol. 1: 32
Washington Post, Vol. 5: 124
Watergate
    Vol. 3: 126
    Vol. 5: 89, 96, 116
Watson-Wentworth, Charles,
    Vol. 1: 73
WCTU. See Women's Christian
    Temperance Union
Webb-Kenyon Act, Vol. 4:
    101–102
Webster, Daniel, Vol. 3: 28, 29,
    30, 38–39, 39
Weddington, Sarah, Vol. 5: 66, 72
Weinberger, Caspar, Vol. 5: 95
Weiner, Mark S., Vol. 5: 123
Weiner, Susan, Vol. 5: 123
Weld, Angelina Grimké, Vol. 3: 53
Weld, Theodore, Vol. 2: 121
Wesley, John, Vol. 2: 115
western lands, Vol. 1: 110–111
Wheeler, Wayne, Vol. 4: 103
Wheeler, William A., Vol. 4: 13
Whig Party, Vol. 3: 35, 38–40,
    47–50, 67–69
"Whiskey Rebellion," Vol. 4: 100
White, Byron, Vol. 5: 72
White, Dexter, Vol. 5: 28
White, Mark, Vol. 5: 128
White, Samuel, Vol. 2: 48
Whitefield, George,
    Vol. 1: 63–65, 64
Whitewater investigation, Vol. 5:
    112–113

Whitman, Walt, Vol. 4: 22
Wilhelm II, Kaiser of Germany,
    Vol. 4: 84
Wilkinson, James, Vol. 2: 54–55
Williams, Roger, Vol. 1: 12–20, 29
Williams, William, Vol. 1: 106
Wilmot, David, Vol. 3: 69
Wilmot Proviso, Vol. 3: 69–70
Wilson, James, Vol. 1: 122
Wilson, Woodrow
    Vol. 4:
        League of Nations and,
            90–94, 96, 97, 97–98
        suffragist movement and,
            113, 115, 117
        World War I and, 81, 82,
            84–85, 88, 92
Wirt, William, Vol. 2: 60
witch trials, Salem,
    Vol. 1: 42–50, 46, 48
Witherspoon, John, Vol. 1: 109
women
    Vol. 2: 99–100, 102
    Vol. 4: 110–120, 114, 117
    Vol. 5: 76, 76–86, 80, 84.
        See also Seneca Falls
        Convention
Women's Christian Temperance
    Union (WCTU), Vol. 4: 101,
    112
Women's Political Union (WPU),
    Vol. 4: 113
Wonders of the Invisible World
    (Mather), Vol. 1: 49
workers, Vol. 4: 73–75,
    77–78, 123
workers rights, Vol. 2: 99–100
Workingman's Party,
    Vol. 4: 35, 37, 37, 38
Works Progress Administration
    (WPA), Vol. 4: 126, 127
World Anti-Slavery Convention,
    Vol. 3: 53–54
World (newspaper), Vol. 4: 60
World War I, Vol. 4: 80–88, 83,
    84, 86, 102–103, 115, 117, 125
World War II, Vol. 5: 13, 13–22,
    15, 21, 24
WPA. See Works Progress
    Administration
WPU. See Women's Political
    Union
Wyoming
    Vol. 3: 59
    Vol. 4: 111

X
XYZ affair, Vol. 2: 23, 24

Y
Yalta Conference, Vol. 5: 28
Yates, Robert, Vol. 1: 130
yellow journalism, Vol. 4: 60

Z
Zenger, John Peter, Vol. 1: 53–58
Zenger trial, Vol. 1: 52–58, 54, 57
Zimmerman, Arthur, Vol. 4: 82